Also by William Jay Smith

POETRY

Poems • Celebration at Dark • Poems
1947-1957 • The Tin Can and Other
Poems • New & Selected Poems • Venice
in the Fog • Journey to the Dead Sea
(FOR CHILDREN) Laughing Time • Boy Blue's
Book of Beasts • Puptents and Pebbles •
Typewriter Town • What Did I See? • Big
and Little: *Little Dimity, Big Gumbo, Big and
Little* • Ho for a Hat! • If I Had a Boat •
Mr. Smith and Other Nonsense • Laughing
Time, Nonsense Poems

AUTOBIOGRAPHY

Army Brat, A Memoir

TRANSLATIONS

Poems of a Multimillionaire, by Valery
Larbaud • Selected Writings of Jules
Laforgue • (FOR CHILDREN) The Children of
the Forest, by Elsa Beskow • The Pirate
Book, by Lennart Hellsing • Two Plays, by
Charles Bertin: *Christopher Columbus* and
Don Juan

CRITICISM

The Spectra Hoax • Herrick, *Selected with
an Introduction and Notes* • Light Verse and
Satires of Witter Bynner, *Edited and with an
Introduction*

ANTHOLOGIES

(with Louise Bogan) The Golden Journey:
Poems for Young People • Poems from France •
Poems from Italy

THE TRAVELER'S TREE

THE TRAVELER'S TREE

New and Selected Poems
by WILLIAM JAY SMITH

Woodcuts by Jacques Hnizdovsky

Persea Books
New York

ACKNOWLEDGMENTS

"Hull Bay, St. Thomas," "Winter Morning," "Fishing for Albacore," and "What Train Will Come?" appeared in *New and Selected Poems*, Seymour Lawrence/Delacorte, 1970; all the other poems and translations in Part One, with the exception of "The Floor and the Ceiling" and "Mr. Smith," are uncollected and most of them have been completed since 1970. Some of them have appeared in the following books and magazines:

Venice in the Fog, The Unicorn Press, 1975; *Journey to the Dead Sea*, Abattoir Editions, 1979, *The Tall Poets*, Palaemon Press, 1979; *Nostalgia for the Present* by Andrei Voznesensky, Doubleday and Company, 1978; *Modern Hungarian Poetry*, edited by Miklós Vajda, Columbia University Press, 1977; and *The Massachusetts Review, The New York Times, The New Republic, The New Hungarian Quarterly, Poetry, Poetry New Paltz, Saturday Review, Shenandoah, The Southern Review, Translation, Vanderbilt Poetry Review*.

"Mr. Smith," "Rear Vision," "A Room in the Villa," "Morels," "Winter Morning," "Hull Bay, St. Thomas," and "Chairs Above the Danube" appeared originally in *The New Yorker*.

The poems in Part Two, "Of Islands," appeared in *Poems* (The Banyan Press, 1947); those in "Celebration at Dark," in *Celebration at Dark* (Farrar, Straus & Giroux, 1950); those in "The Descent of Orpheus," in *Poems 1947-1957* (Atlantic-Little, Brown, 1957); and those in "The Tin Can" in *The Tin Can and Other Poems* (Seymour Lawrence/Delacorte, 1966).

The two stanzas of "You, Andrew Marvell," by Archibald MacLeish are from *New and Collected Poems 1917–1976*, by Archibald MacLeish, published by Houghton Mifflin Company, copyright © 1976 by Archibald MacLeish. Reprinted by permission.

For information, address the publisher:
    Persea Books, Inc.
    225 Lafayette Street
    New York, New York 10012

ISBN: deluxe, limited edition, 0-89255-048-1
    cloth, 0-89255-049-X
    paper, 0-89255-051-1

Library of Congress Catalog Card Number:
    deluxe, limited edition, 80-82587
    cloth, 80-82586

Printed in the United States of America
First Edition

PS3537
.M8693
T7

CONTENTS

Part One

WHAT TRAIN WILL COME?

JOURNEY TO THE DEAD SEA

THE TRAVELER'S TREE

THE TALL POETS

CHAIRS ABOVE THE DANUBE: *Translations*

Part Two

To
Sonja

THE TRAVELER'S TREE

And Spain go under and the shore
Of Africa the gilded sand
And evening vanish and no more
The low pale light across that land

Nor now the long light on the sea—
And here face downward in the sun
To feel how swift how secretly
The shadow of the night comes on...

    —Archibald MacLeish, "You, Andrew Marvell"

Part One

WHAT TRAIN WILL COME?

HULL BAY, ST. THOMAS

For Jay and Ann Logan

We come, with a busload of children, nervous from the heat, down
    through lush vegetation, green from recent rain,

Down from Drake's Seat, from which the explorer must have seen
    the other Virgin Islands as they are now, perched below him
    in blue-green water,

Past palmetto, banana, and brown-podded flamboyant, down to
    cool, yellow-brown sand under a mango tree;

And the children flee from the bus and fan out, a scattering of
    hot seed, over the sand;

Come to a scene straight from an old print, black rocks jumbled
    and jutting ahead into the sky,

A full red sun setting slightly to the left of the rocks, the bay
    fringed with a steady surf, dark above, white beneath,

Spray flung back at the far corners of blue-black rock amid an
    unravelling of pink clouds;

And all that is missing is a high-prowed frigate anchored in the
    foreground, sails furled, its armored captain stepping
    daintily into his boat;

The children, lost sight of like the absent frigate, find
    their own abandoned boat high on the sand under the mango,
    and tumble over its gun-gray gunwales like exhausted birds;

Their cries are muffled by the sound of birds sweeping through
    the air, gliding slowly in, plopping onto the water,

Pelicans with ludicrous long beaks like tilted shears, or, half-
    opened, like garden trowels escaped from the hands of a
    mad gardener,

Pelicans circling, diving—one, two, three at a time—the
    silly beak become a blade,

A surgeon's scalpel, expertly wielded, cutting through the
    delicate green flesh of the water right to the fish below—

Past the snorkeler who comes up gasping for air in the agitated
water—

Beak, body, wings spelling out proudly U-O-M—as Dante saw it
written—MAN in his own language—unmistakably and
violently on the air,

While the children stare from their boat as from a Russian sleigh,
the darkening sand blown before them like snow,

The sun, askew, a blob of red quickly cut from Christmas paper,
the prow of the boat dividing nothing but the oncoming night.

WINTER MORNING

All night the wind swept over the house
And through our dream,
Swirling the snow up through the pines,
Ruffling the white, ice-capped clapboards,
Rattling the windows,
Rustling around and below our bed
So that we rode
Over wild water
In a white ship breasting the waves.
We rode through the night
On green, marbled
Water, and, half-waking, watched
The white, eroded peaks of icebergs
Sail past our windows;
Rode out the night in that north country,
And awoke, the house buried in snow,
Perched on a
Chill promontory, a
Giant's tooth
In the mouth of the cold valley,
Its white tongue looped frozen around us,
The trunks of tall birches
Revealing the rib cage of a whale
Stranded by a still stream;
And saw, through the motionless baleen of their branches,
As if through time,
Light that shone
On a landscape of ivory,
A harbor of bone.

ON THE EDGE

For Gregory on his twenty-first birthday

I

On autumn days when the sky behind
The Vermont mountain opened into a giant gray-blue
Clam shell over us, and birches
By the disjointed skeleton of an old wall
Rose like the thin white spotted legs
Of dangling puppets
We went out to gather mushrooms.
You walked beside me bird-quick, springing
Over wet leaves past the delicate deadly
Amanitas so new and orange-flushed
They seemed to breathe. You crept by them under
A heavy pine branch edged with mist
To pick the ruddy nub of the boletus—
Reaching where I could not reach—
And you were my own arm extending into time,
Bringing reality close up,
Giving color and dimension to the day.

II

On the edge of manhood I found you in an Austrian hotel,
Strong and tall, your black eyes commanding the scene:
You had come down from that higher mountain where
In thin transparent air
Your senses played you false
And the couple on the ledge a mile away
Seemed near enough to touch, the cowbell
On the distant mountain rang next to your ear,
Crisp in the Alpine stillness.

III

There your gaze was true, and you reached
Out to steady me,
Who had tried with you to find

8

The brother and the son who had lost his way,
Fleeing through hemlock-shaded hollows...
And you steadied me that day
Beside a chasm I had barely crossed
Where in a darkening wood below
Pointed fir trees ringed the evening light
And a few stars rose in a clear line
To guide a young man lost.

ELEGY FOR A YOUNG ACTOR

In a gray New England college town
he was handsome and young
and he played the world for all it was worth,
investing each attempted role
with a spendthrift soul.

Poor in the classroom, poor on the boards,
with a voice that seldom could persuade,
but he won us all when he took the lead
in *The Man with the Flower in His Mouth.*
How his black eyes danced;
how he moved with grace
in light as it peeled the fuzz from his cheek
for one whole week!
How we clapped for him then,
for the cut of his clothes,
and the words that rose
from the depth of his youth!

The curtain came down: one summer day
he took the hand of his leading lady,
a tough little blonde;
together they bowed and moved away.

Five years went by, and then he was back,
his life a wreck,
the tough blonde wife holed up in Back Bay
with the director of another play,
and his parents had long since written him off.

The brilliant lighting now had died,
a curtain had gone down inside.
He strode each day to the liquor store,
his face like the paper bag he bore,
wattled and brown,
to his dim little flat on the edge of town.

And then one morning in less than a year
when he did not appear,
no notices went up,
no flowers arrived,
to mark the end of a failed career.

Lord, I know that the worst
is yet to come, but still I mourn
those who are doomed, cursed
from the start,
who can play but one part,
whose every conscious hour is bleak,
the alcoholic, the addict, and the freak,
the actor who makes it for one week.
I mourn their spooned-out lives, their hobbled youth.
And now while a light snow settles like oblivion
on the graveyard of a gray New England town,
I kneel to place,
in memory, one single-petaled, pink, wild rose
in that young actor's mouth.

FISHING FOR ALBACORE

I

Past oil derricks, gray docks, intricate layout of oil pipes, search-
lights wheeling overhead, oil rigs working in darkness with
the motion of praying mantises,

Through gray streets, at 10:00 p.m., down to Pierpont Landing,
Long Beach, where, in the window of a shop offering every
type of fishing gear,

Are displayed fish carved from driftwood by the natives of Bali,
each representing in true colors and exact dimensions a fish
found on their reefs,

Colors derived from bark and root (each fish, when completed, is
bartered for rice; no money is involved);

Then to the Pier, where sixty anglers wait, a bobbing bamboo
wood, to board the Liberty, eighty-five feet long, twenty-
three foot beam, twin diesels, twin stacks painted red, white,
and blue;

And the bamboo surges forward, rustling as in a slow wind, up
the gangplank.

We sail at eleven; stand the poles against the bulkheads, and line
up for rotation tags, my ten-year-old son and I—

Far from those mountains, where, in clear, shallow streams, slim,
speckled trout flicker through massive shadows—

Sail out into San Pedro Bay—Long Beach, San Pedro, Wilmington,
and below, Huntington Beach and Newport Beach,

Spreading behind us their red, green, and yellow fan of light, while
one pale blue searchlight, directed from the city's center,
draws customers to a used car lot;

On until we pull alongside a boat to pick up our live bait, thousands
of anchovies, handed from a wide brown net, in small dipnets
on long aluminum poles,

Anchovy-colored, manipulated deftly like giant darning needles,
anchovies threaded through the nets, dropping into the tanks;

On past the lighthouse, out through the breakwater, where,
behind us, lit-up oil rigs perched in oily water are grotesque
festive birds.

Passengers secure their gear; we seek out our bunks below while
the boat plows ahead into black San Pedro Channel.

We toss for an hour, rough blankets up to our chins, then my son
wakes me, needing air,

And we climb back on deck, proceed to the bow, where water is
played out like the scalloped inside of a shell;

Phosphorescence breaks, has broken, into glowing bits of foam
and then the foam bursts into sprays of flying fish drawn to
the light;

Our wake swerves into a thousand foaming wings; and then,
where the waves rise and fall, two waves break, and then two
more, greener than green,

Not waves but porpoises, darting in and out; the high prow rides
as if harnessed by dolphins, and my son's head on my shoulder,
we fly through the night.

II

Below again. 5:00 a.m.; the engines pause, and groggy, back up: far
off to starboard, an island rides in the water, a carrier;

We sit in the galley and wait, or weave along the decks, following
the flying fish, until dawn, and gray water breaks against
gray sky.

8:00 a.m. We stop; rag lures sweep astern; the crew stands aft,
chumming, tossing dipnets of anchovies into the sea to lure
the albacore—if there are albacore—alongside.

And I picture that fish, dark blue above, shading into smoky silver
below, built for great speed, all its fins fitted and grooved, so
that stream-lined, steel-blue,

13

It makes its way in less than a year between Mexico and Japan; and its spawning grounds are unknown, although one was found once with ripening ovaries in the late summer off Hawaii,—

The long-winged tuna, *Thunnus alalunga,* esteemed for its white flesh, weighing up to forty pounds and a real fighter, taking a trolled lure at eight to ten miles an hour,

That fish the Arabs named *al bukr,* "young camel," of the sea, watching it weave, blue-humped, with long pectoral fins, through warm water.

A strike astern; one of the crewmen reels in, and it *is* an albacore; all sixty poles go over the side, and the deck palpitates with poles, lines bobbing, weaving, thread tangling;

The waves boil with albacore: fat white bellies, long fins sweeping up and down in green water and through the school race the sharks, bloodhounds, blue-green, and the next albacore comes in, a great chunk chewed from its gut.

The captain fires a shot through the poles to kill the scavenger while the bloody fish flops his bloated half-belly on the deck with a hollow gourdlike drumming, and blood runs between our feet;

Still the poles bend and the fish come in; albacore swoop down, away, lines play out;

The cry, "Color!" from every side; deckhands rush up with gaffs, white gasping bodies are hoisted on deck, lines tangle;

Blood on deck, blood in the scuppers, blood and color—"Color!"— and a fat Japanese boy slips in blood, a fat-bellied fish throbbing at his feet;

And through the bamboo forest the sun beats, the sea boils, tempers break with breaking lines; gulls sweep over the bloody blue-green, churning cauldron of the sea.

III

After an hour we rotate positions, moving up toward the bow along the boat's striped divisions.

My son gets a strike; I follow him forward, the pole seeming to grow from his body, and past the other poles I follow his tense face

As he dips with the weight of the fish, bobbing, a bright-painted Russian doll, and I bend to help him steady the pole

And slowly he winds in his prize, boat throbbing, wild water thrashing

Boat heaves, pole heaves, blood on water, blood on deck, on clothes, and steady, slowly, in...

And there he is—"Color!"—right at the prow where the porpoises had guided us through the night

And the deckhand with his gaff hoists an albacore more than half the size of my son, thrashing and throbbing, its dark eye gazing up and out like a button unthreaded and cut.

IV

Hours pass: fish piling up, sun beating down, blood flowing; the school of albacore somewhere behind us,

The anglers, winded now, sprawling, the Liberty skims along, giving form to a formless ocean.

Off to port, sudden activity—not albacore, but waterspouts, a pod of whales...

I think of those young Leviathan amours, that harem and its lord in their indolent rambling, and there somewhere among them, tail to head, all ready for the final spring, the unborn whale lying bent like a Tartar's bow...

Silence...diesel-smell, fish-smell, salt-smell, slip-slap of waves, the afternoon sun drawing into its wrinkled round all the blood of the waves.

We speed back to harbor: the boat become a factory, crewmen aft cleaning fish, blood blowing, hoses running...

Throbbing of engines, gulls following, sun riding, winking low, ribbons of light trailing the horizon,

Waves changing, gray, blue-green, orange, gray, and then the whole surface weighted, leaden,

Until night comes down, and a semicircle of light dances before us, and we whip through the channel, past the lighthouse, a squat owl in black water,

Back to the Pier, the blue searchlight spanning the sky, oil rigs pumping in the dark, cold light sweeping the Liberty as she eases in;

And then, plumped down on the pier, in sacks, one hundred twenty albacore, whose steel-blue bodies will no longer flash on that mysterious migration,

Through that boiling ocean, past whales coupling in foaming water, resting mid-earth in the green wavering circle of their families,

And we come down to the dock, in hot light, past skeletal poles, raw laughter, lights flashing—

Come there to my mother who waits proudly to greet us; and then one bright, final flash against the gray (her camera), and there, in a circle of light,

As on some permanent atoll, I see my son, smiling, holding his fish, reflected, blue and silver, in my mother's eyes.

WHAT TRAIN WILL COME?

For Jack and Marty Hall
What train will come to bear me back across so wide a town?
      —found scrawled in a subway station

Snow drifts melt in the streets, pock-marked at the curb
      as by newsprint, and the wind whips up the snow; the air tastes
      of black foam;

The world becomes a wet newspaper into whose blown pages now
      I step, snow mounting all around,

Smudged white walls where howling newsprint peels, tooth-white
      crevasses on which graffiti dance.

The wet dark rushes up as I descend where the black turnstile
      rests, an upended propeller,

And the steps at the edge of the platform echo as if from
      another deserted platform toward another on and on

Like the tapping of miners through the dark; and my heel clicks
      in the cold on a toothless silver comb...

What train will come?

Wet clings to my body; gray ash sifts down upon the track
      unwinding ahead, and I can hear far off—or is it far off in the
      mind?—the clang of car on car,

The human chain, the haunted sound; and before me a broken
      mirror swings in the void at the track's edge

And through it cracks spread from a dark center—veins
      like roots tunnelling through the ground—

And my step clicks on cement, and whichever way I move—from
      whichever way the train will come—the way is down...

While wheels—remembered wheels—turn dizzily before me
      with the broken glass

And in the glass a face that in the silence spreads and turns;
      and in my chest a heart-beat like a distant drum...

17

What train will come?

Glass glints; shoe creaks...A small child, I walked after
  a tornado in the city, holding my mother's hand,

The sky open again above us like a wound drained of blood, the
  pale edges folded in upon a pink center;

I strolled beside her, and she seemed to spin off from me in
  her dress of voile, her cartwheel hat;

And I gazed out on tilted and shattered telephone poles, their
  wires trailing over sidewalks like black spaghetti;

An acrid taste of burning bread hovered in the air; the most
  intimate parts of buildings had been ripped off, and here
  a bed dangled down

And there was the smell of buried flesh; and I was sick and
  wanted to hide my face and run to some green spot, gaze up
  at a proper sun-lit dome...

What train will come?

O violent earth: I think of the morning Darwin saw you,
  "the very emblem of all that is solid," a world

That had moved overnight beneath his feet "like a crust over
  a fluid," and when he sailed into Talcahuano Bay

All was strangely still: after the battering waves, water black and
  boiling where the seabed had seemed to crack open;

The shore was strewn with debris, ships keeling over on a
  plain of mud and soggy seaweed,

Burst cotton bales, dead animals, uprooted trees, housetops
  lay tossed about and huge rocks covered the beaches;

And there had been little warning: the first shocks, and then
  the curious twisting movement, making the ground open and
  then close again—as on a tomb...

18

What train will come?

But now we do not wait: we rip the earth apart ourselves,
    bulldoze the dead before us,

Make a desert of our blue earth, and explore the desert moon,
    bringing

Her rocks to add to those we pile upon our dead, while in an
    empty landscape of slag heaps

And smoking lagoons the black poor gather under a low sky, and
    trapped light hovers like false dawn;

The assassin's bullet is answered by a quiet voice: "Put
    your banners down; go quietly home..."

And another bullet answers; and still the banners rage and
    blaze and burn: Which way is back? Which way is home?

What train will come?

Violence breeds violence until the chain binds and slashes
    over burned-over ground

And the distant war is brought closer, diminished on the TV
    screen: men kill men, and all three inches tall...

In a small skirmish—"little activity, two or three dead,
    nothing extraordinary,"

In a country that is soft and wet and hot; now under whirling
    chopper blades the grass huts blaze

And the little moon-faced people are lined up for a roll of
    color film—men, women, children—and shot down

And with cadaver obedience heaped by rice paddy and rubble—
    all to be neatly held one day upon a screen within a frame
    of chrome...

What train will come?

Three inches tall (in memory) I wander up and down...Ah,
    once I loved a stone, the shape of water winding through

Wild rose, sweet william, Indian paint brush, and in the woods
    a woman (was it my mother?) walking in yellow lace

Through violet shadows, nodding and talking...And I left her
    there by the stream...and then that night found her again

Locked in a little room at the top of the stairs, moaning and
    calling as if from underground,

And the club that had beaten her rested like some heraldic
    emblem beside the door where the drunken man had placed it;

And I knelt down, staring into my own vomit, helpless, dazed,
    and dumb...

What train will come?

O dreadful night!...What train will come?...What tree is
    that?...a sycamore—the mottled bark stripped bare,

Desolate in winter light against the track, and I continue
    on to the mudflats

By the roaring river where garbage, chicken coops, and houses
    rush by me on mud-crested waves,

And at my feet are dead fish—catfish, gars—and there in a
    little inlet

Come on a deserted camp, the tin can in which the hoboes brewed
    their coffee stained bitter black

As the cinders sweeping ahead under a milkweed-colored sky
    along a darkening track

    And gaze into a slough's green stagnant foam,
        and know that the way out is never back,

            but down,

                down...

What train will come

to bear me back

across so wide a town?

JOURNEY TO THE DEAD SEA

AT DELPHI

For Allen Tate on his seventy-fifth birthday

I

This morning on the edge of Parnassus we watched the old women
    at Arakhova, where the houses

Rise in terraces on the mountain spur, black kerchiefs knotted
    at their throats,

Holding spools of cotton in their crooked hands like the unformed
    substance of life

Itself, drawing the thread out from below, whipping it in blue
    light through agile fingers;

That thread has followed us throughout the day at Delphi among
    the ruins,

Cicadas stitching the dry air, which Plutarch found "close and
    compact

With a tenseness caused by reflection of the mountains and their
    resistance,

But at the same time fine and biting... as fine and close
    as silk;"

Has followed us past temple, treasury, theatre, and stadium to the
    edge of that spring

Separating with its white tongue the twin Phaeriades, the Shining
    Rocks,

Where in niches above green water black and white butterflies,
    their wings

Patterned like ancient pottery, hovered in the heat; has followed
    us to that oval

Spindle-plaited stone that marked the place where those two
    eagles released

By Zeus—one from the east and one from the west—once met, to
    that

Omphalos, cut and tied by the legendary Earth-mother, to the
navel of the world.

II

Far from this earth center, guarded by the python coiling from its
seismic chasm

To the hot dry Kentucky of your youth, where "long shadows of
grapevine wriggle and run over the green swirl,"

Far from the tulip tree and the creek road winding under the
quicksilver sky,

Where the drowsing copperhead kept watch beside the water "that
bells and bickers

All night long," far from that shaded path beside the swimming-
hole, where you saw

The black man's body fallen from the tree, and saw it dragged
unclaimed

Into the town, far from that clear spring of love that broke through
multiple

Layers of memory to recreate that scene and find that the central
evil of this earth

May be redeemed in art, as here within a frame of sculpted
palmette and lotus

Mythic scenes depict a continuing triumph against barbarian
invaders; I think of you

And of your victory now while cicadas echo through the valley,
and the twin reflecting rocks

Reflect the pink and amber light, down the darkening precipice as
far as the mirroring

Sea of Corinth, and the olive trees below us here take on the
verdigris of a great

Bronze shield deposited on the stone-ribbed slope in an ancient
    battle between giants.

III

The thread of light unwinds around the cypresses like blue-black
    spools,

Along the gold-green edges of pine needles; and bats sweep forth
    as if released

On thread, skimming, dipping, knitting together the last frayed
    patches

Of light. Parnassus draws in upon itself, and in the pit-stillness
    now I hear

A voice asking: "Who among you doubts whether thunder sends
    forth a voice?"

And now hear thunder breaking like clear water from the rocks,
    and hear

The oracle speak again from out the centuries, its message clear
    and understood:

"What can survive this light if it is not language?" and hear as
    in your poem

Hoofbeats resounding on a dim and dusty road; and now the
    cicadas cease;

The night draws fully in, thread over fine, thin fingers at the
    center of the earth.

VENICE IN THE FOG

For Sonja, con amore

I

Fog in mid-December has descended on Venice; and the city wraps itself around itself

Like the seahorses we have seen in the aquarium, tails linked, twisting, turning,

Rising gently to the green surface of the water; the water of Venice, a mirror,

Is held up on all sides so that the bridge reflected rises and drifts toward us, a twisted turret,

And the city, lighter than goose down, is about to float through the air—

Or rest, a hulk, a battleship stranded, gray on gray sand, green barnacles encrusting

Its gray guns; the silver of the mirror is rubbed away so that one looks not into, but through, the glass,

And moves in a carnival, where black masks wander up and down, and the people wearing them

Are nowhere to be seen—they're lost in fog—and the buildings come at you through holes in the masks;

Bodies—ghosts' bodies—brush by you in the mist; the Bridge of Sighs is an eyelid

Lifted on a gray eyeball; and behind it a red boat light slowly streaks with blood.

II

St. Mark's bursts at us through fog, the mottled, humped face of a bright tropical fish;

The Doge's Palace beside it rests on the intaglio of its pillars, a stranded fish skeleton.

The *acqua alta* has subsided; in dim pools in the square the pigeons huddle in the cold,

Flying apart of a sudden like a fringe of wool, purple threads at their throats,

And one, frayed and battered, limps off toward the ruby glow of a jeweled shop,

And, nuzzling its head against a column, falls over dead, its mauve feathers the wet wisps of an old broom.

Fragments of buildings—architraves, cornices, pediments—fly through the night

And here at our feet, a group of gondolas tied together sit, squat, a row of black, muzzled dogs.

The lighted shops are so many bright boxes spilling out into the night—gold, glass beads

Falling beside the water like multiple chains from the throats of Venetian women.

Now in La Fenice—the fog behind us—we are inside the golden box, and below us women in Minoan dress

Sing out their lives, and fall spent on amber rocks...And now pink lobster, eel,

Layers of encrusted crayfish swim toward us through the gray light where streetlights drift,

The blue-pink pods of the medusa...And our forks come down upon the plate,

Cutting through the fog; we begin to bite into Venice, tasting its hidden, sea-green sweetness.

III

Three days and the fog gives no sign of lifting (after three days of fog it rains, they tell us)...

Cats go masked; white-veiled, bulging flower shops float off,
barges bearing the remnants

Of bridal festivities ... I touch their perfume as they move
away; and from here in the room gaze down

On the bridge below and the shops beside it held in marbled water,
veins of mist cutting

Through it while my pen on the page cuts through veined layers
of consciousness ...

Domes, arched windows rising toward me are bushes bent down
with snow and ice; and the saints from their niches

Fly out like birds, all saying: Life is neither nightmare nor dream
but dream and reality converging;

Heaven, as Blake knew, can be met with anywhere, and what
cannot be seen must be imagined and seen more clearly ...

Here seven years ago I walked at night through the fog, my steps
echoing behind me;

My past life rose up unmasked before me; and even then I could
see your face—a face I had not yet seen—

Swim toward me—a bright fine-boned face parting the spray
before it, the figurehead of a ship ...

And I gaze down now into the fog, and hear behind me—echoing
up through my life—

Your steps on the stair; you come in, cold from your walk, and
toss your purple cape on the bed, its fur wet from the fog;

Your hair falls red about your throat; you turn from the gold room
and run the water in the bath,

Steam rising from it like fog; and below me footsteps echo on the
pavement; bell buoys clang in the distance ...

You step from your warm bath and lie down beside me; my hand
moves over the nipples of your breast,

Down over the firm belly and rests on your thigh; as the mirror
breaks in a thousand pieces,

The room is all pomegranate and gold; the fog clears—parting
as if for the marriage of Venice with the sea—

And all that could not be seen is seen, all that was imagined, is, all
that was lost, found.

JOURNEY TO THE DEAD SEA

> Fishermen will stand beside the sea; from En-gedi to En-eglaim it
> will be a place for the spreading of nets; its fish will be of very many
> kinds, like the fish of the Great Sea.... And on the banks, on both
> sides of the river, there will grow all kinds of trees for food. Their
> leaves will not wither nor their fruit fail, but they will bear fresh
> fruit every month, because the water for them flows from the sanc-
> tuary. Their fruit will be for food and their leaves for healing.
> —*Ezekiel 47:10-12*

For Robert Penn Warren

I

On the outskirts of Tel Aviv a dromedary is chained in a vacant lot
    near a junkyard,
And soon the orange groves begin: on the right, a railroad to the
    Gaza strip,
A highway to bring potash to Ashdod; on the left, the mountains
    of Judah.
Our bus driver maneuvers, stares ahead; in the green frog-goggles
    of our guide pass
Rows of eucalyptus, pecan plantations; he drones on from under
    his baseball cap:
"And so in 1946 the Jews built eleven villages overnight, for by
    Turkish law
Dwelling was occupation, and the British must respect what
    was done..."
His accent thick as German pickles, his tongue heavy on each
    syllable, he squats
Before us, cap twisted to one side, as if ready to shuffle into some
    burlesque routine,
His jokes as old as time, as alive as the weather, survivor of Buchen-
    wald, green-checked and goggled.
"Each country has its problem. We have our problem. Who is a
    Jew? What is a Jew?...
In Haifa," he booms, "the cinemas are closing; they're turning into
    wedding halls..."
And his voice reaches back over the shaded green seats, coming
    not from the loudspeaker

But rising, dark life-force, from time itself. Life, it seems to say,
    is there to be enjoyed;
And I am that fool in the legend who guides you on all your
    journeys back
Into yourself, who takes his own long journey back to his village,
    and looks up
At his native sky, saying, I have traveled far, but to this final place
    I come
Where the sky is as clear as it was in my own village; this is my
    place; here I am home.

II

And here the descent begins: after dusty Beersheba with its
    hibiscus and pepper trees,
Where, in the dark hotel interior, pink roses rest frozen in wax,
    and olives have the cold flavor of underground
Wells, Beersheba, where early each morning the Bedouins come to
    bargain
For dromedaries; after Dimonah, in Hebrew "wasting," where the
    sewage water
Is used and reused; after a textile factory, a domed atomic reactor
    perched
Like a mosque in the distance, the desert begins, breaks off in
    pieces—
The hills break off—and there three gasoline drums, rusting
    below us,
Are tucked between boulders; and down the slope a piece of flint
    flicking the heat,
A gazelle. We wind down past the carcass of a junked car robin's-
    egg blue,
And the heat wavers, rests in folds of rock; wind down through
    earth's deepest depression,
Down through the cut—the *ghor*—there to a curve, where the bus
    draws up
Beside a rust-red overturned truck where tourists are eating
    watermelon, its wet red flesh

Blood dripping among boulders, its black seed scattered around them like dim

Figures of Bedouins disappearing in the heat; and we gaze out through shimmering heat waves,

White salt smoke pouring upward in newly-hatched green insect stripes—

Where does land stop and sea begin?—gaze out through heat more visible

Than a mirage upon that fabled Salt Sea, *Yam Ha-Melach,* stretching north and south,

Sea of Lot, *Bahr Lut,* the Eastern Sea, Sea of Overwhelming, Sea of the Plain,

Sea of the Arabah, Dead Sea, *Lacus Asphaltites,* Lake of Bitumin, ten miles across,

Forty-six miles long, the stagnant green surface lying thirteen hundred feet below the Mediterranean,

And thirteen hundred feet deep—gaze out on the thick, gassy, bitter waters

In which no fish live, over which no birds fly; where the ancient traveler saw

No plants rising in the poisonous air along the shore but forests of legendary pine

In its green depth, and, wavering among them, the burnt, scarred, toppled towers of the Cities of Plain.

III

No birds, no fish; but the valley is a fish skeleton, the striated rib cage

Of a whale, which we enter, skirting green decaying flesh flaking off through the air—

Fresh water rising in vapor along the blazing rocks lining wind-worn wadies—

The white marl of *Al Lisan,* the tongue, dividing the green surface— the mucus-like basins

Of the bromide factories, where green water is made greener to hasten evaporation—

On through hallucinatory green—to Mount Sodom, where a
 huge squat rock figure—
Wind-ruffled and worn, looking like Queen Victoria surveying
 her dead domain—Mrs. Lot, our guide tells us,
Who, not obeying her master, has become a salt pillar; and then
 Mesada, cut off by two wadies,
Perched where blue-white clouds form over the valley—a final
 refuge
After the fall of Jerusalem, where nine hundred and sixty-seven
 Jews chose suicide rather than surrender—
Their ghosts for centuries circling the yellow outcroppings on the
 plateau of Judea,
Where, as at Auschwitz, "a clear sky spreads over the shaven
 skulls," and, below, at Kallia
We enter the sea itself, six times saltier than any ocean: the bus, in
 a flood-lit nightmare,
Discharges its odd passengers on the hot shore: the mouse-man
 from Detroit, the eaglet sculptress from California,
A red bandanna knotted round her head, the prim straw-hatted
 duck from Brooklyn, the dodo, the jay—
All bobbing in grease-thick water up to our armpits below tooth-
 pick telephone poles
Receding in the distance—under the green-goggled eyes of our
 guide—
Afloat in this interior ocean salt-scaled, tasting and smelling of
 salt—
The plain of Moab drifting above us like the back of a bloated
 camel at a dried-up waterhole—
Released in an ever-renewed pool of tears at the bottom of the
 world.

IV

In the Bedouin's tent as if high on a camel's hump, tent poles
 slanting and swaying,
We rest in the desert heat: ashes in the center brew coffee while
 earth

Sways with the tent's panels: in memory the afternoon sways,
    sinks and rises—
Draws up that level sunken sea with its twisted salt-coated rocks,
    that glaucous pit
Where death itself appeared to reject us, that sulphurous sea in
    the deep-faulted desert;
And in the shifting fire, its coals like fruits "that tempt the eye,
    but turn to ashes on the lips"—
In the gathering dust of the apples of Sodom—we watch, remem-
    bering, yellow sand move
And from the sand gazelles that clatter down the cliffside; and
    there from some faulted point
Deep in the earth on that inner ear that bears all memory of sound
    imprinted in fossil now breaks
A sudden rush of clear water, falling as from Himalayan heights,
    sweet water cutting through bitter rock
To a desert of thorn trees, to the briars and hollow apples there
    at the edge
Of the Salt Sea, into a brake of rushes and reeds, the oasis of
    En-gedi,
David's green refuge, a place of caverns and strongholds, where
    the soul knows
That in gardens of cucumber and melon it will taste water that
    has worked its hidden
Way through deepest desert, and, touching the planet's most
    poisoned spot,
Falls on a clear cold pool, tilting with stars, encircled with smooth
    rocks and cress,
On that healing place this side of death that can be reached only
    through knowledge and pain.

Boston Public Library

Customer ID: **********5243

Title: Tinkers /
ID: 39999068477957
Due: 06/13/11

Title: The traveler's tree : new and select
ID: 39999040705244
Due: 06/13/11

Total items: 2
5/23/2011 8:28 PM

Thank you for using the
3M SelfCheck™ System.

THE TRAVELER'S TREE

THE TRAVELER'S TREE

Its common name derives from its having hollow bases to its leaf
stalks from which it is said that travelers obtained drinking water.
The traveler's tree has a palmlike trunk up to 30 feet in height and
immense long-stemmed, paddle-shaped leaves arranged in two ranks
spread in one plane like a gigantic fan. Although the leaves do not
naturally divide, they are usually more or less shredded by wind
action.

—Thomas H. Everett, *Living Trees of the World*

I

On a day like this so clear that your eye
can carry you over the beckoning curve of the horizon
you will be lifted slowly on wings that seem
to touch the end of time—
lifted in memory or dream—
and the golden cubes of buildings will settle on green banks
or tumble into the bronze river,
monumental amber pieces from the broken necklace of a giantess:
on such a day in the late afternoon you will begin your journey.

You will travel in a series of perfect ever-present moments,
moments just past that you can never retrieve
and yet will hold forever: you will leave
behind you constant flashing scenes—
sunlight dappling clear spring water
until grasses growing in green depths
surround you of a sudden like a fringe of willows
on a sandbank in midsummer—
and all that had been wavering within is there without.

The world will open then before you; you will move over a snow-
    swirled
landscape, carried along as palpably as snow
that obliterates black rock
and weighs down thick pine branches—
borne along still fjords until you reach a point
where ice breaks off, and you rest on blue water,
and prisms of ice drift past you,
melting with the changing seasons into a quiet sea.

And now you cross that sea: the prow of your ship
cuts through blue-black water with a sound like the tearing of silk,
and phosphor rides in your wake
to the edge of the stars: the great cross
hangs above you on the wrinkled cassock of the south;
and chains of dolphins guide you between shaggy, humpbacked
    islands.

To the left, a light cascades across the sky,
pulsing pink, then red, and deeper red,
the rambling petals of a giant rose gone wild,
flung in profusion down the mountainside:
a volcano that erupts, its rumble muffled by the wind,
its shadow sifting down dustlike on your face and on the waves
until the night explodes in pulsing pink and the ship
in the sea's dark troughs rides, a veering worm,
into the heartbeat of the world become a rose.

II

Through a white coral passage that appears
no wider than your body's width,
you move into a final harbor, an atoll's closed lagoon,
staring into space, the earth's eyeball,
and its clear coral depth contains, the frozen garlands
of former travelers, a lifetime's thoughts,
around which circle striped and spotted fish.
A thousand sea birds, frigates, terns,
weaving, whirling, conduct you to the shore
and to a fronded, mottled path—
through lianas enveloping a rich, decaying vegetation—
to a clearing, where, on a green mound,
little more than a swelling of the ground,
its central opening, a wide, dark mouth rising to catch the wind,
rests the low-lying house.

III

There shoulder-high, the leaves long-stemmed
and paddle-shaped, arranged in two ranks spread
in one plane,
into a wind-shredded, green, gigantic fan—
the turkey headdress of some Cherokee chieftain—
rises the traveler's tree
in white hot light,
trunk resting on the dwarf, ignorant earth,
the many arms of Siva fringed in fire—
life entire—
creator and destroyer, magnificent wild dancer,
whom even the gods lean down to see,
the mystic tree, the traveler's tree.

Break off a branch, a leaf stalk: from its hollow base
drink, as from some deep well of air,
its water, long-collected, cold and clear.
And breaking off that branch, you will break off your dream
and be again a boy in a small boat
drinking from a paddle
the transparent water of a mountain stream.

Then cross the threshold and enter the dark house.
You will be welcome. I will be waiting. I will be there.

THE TALL POETS

THE TALL POETS

A Bicentennial Meditation—July 4, 1976

While the sky above Manhattan flaps with a thousand Jasper Johns,
past file after file of duplicate jubilant faces—
under the glorious gray-green artichoke crown of Liberty,
their free-flowing purple beards catching fire in the morning light
and trailing behind them in wondrous ash-blue wakes
on the welcoming water,
the Tall Poets—in Operation Poetry—
sail up the lordly Hudson.

Manned by the Irish Mafia and the Jewish Mafia
and the Yugoslavian Mafia
(whatever happened to the Sicilian Mafia?)—
a light breeze rippling the fluent free verse of their rigging—
together with the Tall Women Poets,
decked out in tough companionate canvas pants suits,
vulvas cleaving the wind,
the Tall Poets proceed pontifically up the lordly Hudson
on this bright Bicentennial morning.

And there in the mid-Mondrian of Manhattan—
with the boogie-woogie beat of its red white and blue squares—
beside her jade plant and her rubber plant and her Kaffir lily,
beside her innumerable cascading spider plants,
in her Empire chair
beside her Louis Seize commode—
my lady, the lovely long-legged Swan of Strasbourg,
(Yes, Lafayette, she is here)
leans this morning from her white air-conditioned tower,
brooding over the gray water, and she says:

"Where are you, William, why are you not here,
your blue beard billowing above the water,
your majestic *vers libre* ribboning out on the wind—
why are you not here sailing among the Tallest of the Tall Poets—
in Operation Poetry—
up the lordly Hudson?

Why do you dither down there in your dark bayou?
Why do you not let it all hang out
on this bright Bicentennial morning?"

So speaks my beloved, the Swan of Strasbourg,
and I look northward toward her white air-conditioned tower,
and wiping my forehead in the steaming swamp, I answer:
"O my Swan, I wish that I could join you there
in that bright and bugling Bicentennial air—
but my beard, my love,
(the legacy of my Choctaw forebears)
grows solely on my lips and chin
and when it grows I look like Ho Chi Minh
(or did when I was thin)
but now under the TV cameras
my eyebrows disappear—and my beard
becomes a wreath of cobwebs
around a moon-shaped face
until I look like the ghost of Mao Tse-Tung...
How wretched and ridiculous I would appear,
sailing up the lordly Hudson there
on this bright Bicentennial morning!....

"And besides, I am bored with those Tall Poets,
those first and second generation baby Bunyans,
sick of their creatively-written writing,
their blithering buffoonery, their diapered Dada,
their petulant pornography,
their syrupy self-pitying self-interviews,
their admired ash-buried academic anorexia...
I'm weary of having to dive into their driven dreck that hits the fan
weekly in every puffed and pompous periodical....
I long for the pure poem,
the passionate statement,
the simple declarative sentence...
We live in a bad time...and I cannot write...
I paddle around this black bayou in my pirogue...
Spanish moss hangs from the live oaks like the ash of innumerable
    cigarettes,

46

and the cypress knees protrude from the black water
like arthritic fingers above a silent typewriter keyboard....
In the dead silence of the bayou a voice deep within me says:
'Walt Whitman is alive and well, and inhabits the Bronx;
he teaches at Stony Brook, and knows exactly what America is
thinking.
To hell with rhyme and reason! Walt, unwind!...Poor Smith is a
hack
overly enamored of writer's block:
he doesn't even know what he thinks until he's said
it; and he has nothing to say.
His mind is as blank as the wobbly whiskered wall-eyed catfish
that he pulled out of the bayou
on this bright Bicentennial morning.'
So says the inner voice while light creaks
down through the rose windows of the cypresses,
and a woodpecker pecks on the dead wood overhead."

From her white air-conditioned tower the Swan of Strasbourg
speaks:
"Don't be silly. Stop paddling around in your little pirogue.
Get out of the black backwater of that bayou:
come back up here to the lordly Hudson,
and be the Tall Poet God intended you to be.
Join the other Tall Poets.
Magne-toi le popotin! I didn't marry a piddling paddler of pirogues!"

"Swan," I say, "I know that your great-uncle designed those broad
avenues in Paris,
and where would we be, I hesitate to say,
without the Champs Elysées?
But I don't feel a bit monumental this Bicentennial morning...
Come down, my darling, from your white tower; leave your Louis
Seize commode
and your Empire chair and your *Compagnie des Indes* china
behind you: come down here to join me in my pirogue,
and together we shall thread our way through the innumerable
Louisiana bayous
as intricate as the branches of your spider plants—

47

through the land of my birth—past Dugdemona Swamp and
    Saline Lake—
past the *Côte joyeuse* and down the Red River like my forebears
past the bearded oaks and the sagging white columns of the
    plantations
and the writhing black grillwork of Bourbon Street—
through the jubilant notes of early jazz—
and finally out into the glorious Gulf . . . and the light around us
will be pale green—
feathery and fine as stalks of fennel against a background
of mother-of-pearl,
and when we reach a point unknown on any chart,
and I can say with your Racine,
'The day is no less pure than the depth of my heart,'
I shall begin to write again; and I shall complete that poem begun
a lifetime ago on the edge of the great brown river
on an April morning beside a bank of violets—
a poem of life and death, of love and memory:

"While the Tall Poets—in Operation Poetry—sail up the lordly
    Hudson,
past the gray contiguous cliffs of the academies,
into the locked and heavily guarded harbors of the anthologies
on this bright Bicentennial morning."

THREE SONGS

I WORDS BY THE WATER

Beneath the dimming gardens of the sky
That ship, my heart, now rides its anchor chain;
A room is harbor when the world's awry
And life's direction anything but plain.
Still is the wind, and softer still the rain.
Sleep in my arms, my love. O sleep, my love.

Time hangs suspended: with its floating farms,
Its peacock-green and terraced atmosphere,
Now sleep awaits us, love. Lie in my arms;
It is not death but distance that I fear,
Dark is the day, and dangerous the year.
Sleep in my arms, my love. O sleep, my love.

II SONG FOR A COUNTRY WEDDING

For Deborah and Marc

We have come in the winter
To this warm country room,
The family and friends
Of the bride and the groom,
To bring them our blessing,
To share in their joy,
And to hope that years passing
The best measures employ
    To protect their small clearing,
    And their love be enduring.

May the hawk that flies over
These thick-wooded hills,
Where through tangled ground cover
With its cushion of quills
The plump porcupine ambles
And the deer come to browse
While through birches and brambles
Clear cold water flows,
    Protect their small clearing,
    And their love be enduring.

May the green leaves returning
To rock maples in spring
Catch fire, and, still burning,
Their flaming coat fling
On the lovers when sleeping
To contain the first chill
Of crisp autumn weather
With log-fires that will
    Protect their small clearing,
    And their love be enduring.

May the air that grows colder
Where the glacier has left
Its erratic boulder
Mountain water has cleft,
And the snow then descending
No less clear than their love
Be a white quilt depending
From sheer whiteness above
    To protect their small clearing,
    And their love be enduring.

III MOURNING SONG

Comb the haunted, howling seas,
Count the countless railroad ties,
Nail the rivers to the trees:
    The dead have haddocks' eyes.

Void the cranny, scour the plain,
Scale the peak where no winds rise,
Thread the needles of the rain:
    The dead have haddocks' eyes.

Circle skyward, catch your breath,
Net the bird that blinded flies,
Touch the whirling hem of Death:
    The dead have haddocks' eyes.

Close the silken, quilted lid—
The coffin where your father lies,—
Then stare the dark down as he did:
    The dead have haddocks' eyes.

Then stare the dark down: watch the foam
Of swirling breakers fall and rise
To heave the wild-eyed haddock home:
    The dead have haddocks' eyes.

BACHELOR'S-BUTTONS

Bachelor's-buttons are fine to see
When one is unattached and free,

When days are long and cares are few
And every green field sown with blue

Cornflowers that profusely seem
Attendant on a young man's dream.

Bachelor's-buttons are fine to see
When one knows no frugality;

And splendid to behold again
Lacing a jacket of gold grain,

A border tended by a wife
Who mends the fraying edge of life;

Who fashions in a hundred ways
Bright seams that cut through one's dark days;

Or will until buttons are counted and sold,
And the blue thread breaks, and earth is cold.

THE DIVER

Down the dark-skinned diver dived
 In the Indian Ocean of my tear,
Tasted salt, and then drowned.

Coral shades him like a tree
 While overhead the waves pound
Cove and cavern piteously.

Life in contradiction lies,
 And friends are by subtraction found:
The raging water fills my eyes.

EPITAPHS

A LAWYER

In Memoriam Francis Biddle (1886-1968)

In life each man is tried
And judged at life's expense,
And Time that prosecutes
With such cold competence
Will triumph utterly
Over all humanity,
But, oh, in that great court—
All just men will agree—
How brilliant his defense.

A GREENSKEEPER

With patient care and subtlety
He ministered to turf and tree:
Gaze now on his green legacy.

A STRIPPER

Here lies the stripper stripped, disrobed for good;
Death wholly bares what life but partly could.
The house lights dim: each pointed, star-tipped breast
Invites complete approval east and west.

A SMALL DOG

A Lhasa apso that died fighting with a
Saint Bernard on the coast of Maine

Here Fearless lies: with Asian pride,
Longhaired and small, by the oceanside,
He took up the challenge, fought, and died;
Now hear his bark in the rising tide.

THE FLOOR AND THE CEILING

Winter and summer, whatever the weather,
The Floor and Ceiling were happy together
In a quaint little house on the outskirts of town
With the Floor looking up and the Ceiling looking down.

The Floor bought the Ceiling an ostrich-plumed hat,
And they dined upon drippings of bacon fat,
Diced artichoke hearts and cottage cheese
And hundreds of other such delicacies.

On a screened-in porch in early spring
They would sit at the player piano and sing.
When the Floor cried in French, *"Ah, je vous adore!"*
The Ceiling replied, "You adorable Floor!"

The years went by as the years they will,
And each little thing was fine until
One evening, enjoying their bacon fat,
The Floor and the Ceiling had a terrible spat.

The Ceiling, loftily looking down,
Said, "You are the *lowest* Floor in this town!"
The Floor, looking up with a frightening grin,
Said, "Keep up your chatter, and *you* will cave in!"

So they went off to bed: while the Floor settled down,
The Ceiling packed up her gay wallflower gown;
And tiptoeing out past the Chippendale chair
And the gateleg table, down the stair,

Took a coat from the hook and a hat from the rack,
And flew out the door—farewell to the Floor!—
And flew out the door, and was seen no more,
And flew out the door, and *never* came back!

In a quaint little house on the outskirts of town,
Now the shutters go bang, and the walls tumble down;
And the roses in summer run wild through the room,
But blooming for no one—then why should they bloom?

For what is a Floor now that brambles have grown
Over window and woodwork and chimney of stone?
For what is a Floor when the Floor stands alone?
And what is a Ceiling when the Ceiling has flown?

MR. SMITH

How rewarding to know Mr. Smith,
    Whose writings at random appear!
Some think him a joy to be with
    While others do not, it is clear.

His eyes are somewhat Oriental,
    His fingers are notably long;
His disposition is gentle,
    He will jump at the sound of a gong.

His chin is quite smooth and uncleft,
    His face is clean-shaven and bright,
His right arm looks much like his left,
    His left leg it goes with his right.

He has friends in the arts and the sciences;
    He knows only one talent scout;
He can cope with most kitchen appliances,
    But in general prefers dining out.

When young he collected matchboxes,
    He now collects notebooks and hats;
He has eaten *roussettes* (flying foxes),
    Which are really the next thing to bats!

He has never set foot on Majorca,
    He has been to Tahiti twice,
But will seldom, no veteran walker,
    Take two steps when one will suffice.

He abhors motorbikes and boiled cabbage;
    Zippers he just tolerates;
He is wholly indifferent to cribbage,
    And cuts a poor figure on skates.

He weeps by the side of the ocean,
    And goes back the way that he came;
He calls out his name with emotion—
    It returns to him always the same.

It returns on the wind and he hears it
    While the waves make a rustle around;
The dark settles down, and he fears it,
    He fears its thin, crickety sound.

He thinks more and more as time passes,
    Rarely opens a volume on myth.
Until mourned by the tall prairie grasses,
    How rewarding to know Mr. Smith!

CHAIRS ABOVE THE DANUBE
Translations

In these translations I have had the following collaborators: for the Hungarian poems Miklós Vajda, Julia Kada, and Gyula Kodolányi; for the poems of Andrei Voznesensky the author and Vera Dunham; for the poem of Luko Paljetak the author.—W.J.S.

SZABOLCS VÁRADY: CHAIRS ABOVE THE DANUBE

Those two chairs were not really
all that ugly. Too bad the springs
protruded from them and the upholstery
was so hopelessly filthy.

But chairs they were, all the same. And right for that apartment.
So we carried them, mostly on our heads,
from Orlay Street across the former
Francis Joseph, now Liberty, Bridge,
to Number 2 Ráday Street where P. lived
at the time (as some of his poems will show.)

A chair, not to say two, has
many uses. "Two Poets on a Bridge
with Chairs on their Heads"—one can imagine
a painting so entitled. I hope it would be
a down-to-earth painting and not one of those
transfigurations. Those two chairs—
and it's important to make this clear—were by no means
just halos around our heads. About halfway across the bridge—
and not for the purpose of proving anything—
we sat down on them. The springs protruded more prominently
    from
one—I don't recall which of us
got it. Doesn't matter since what happened later
can hardly be explained by that. It was a pleasant
summer evening. We lit cigarettes,
enjoying this one might say
unusual form of coziness.
                    The chairs later served
nicely for a while: at the P.s' they
were *the* chairs. But man wants something better
than what is: the chairs were sent to an upholsterer. Then the P.s
moved also, the first time, because they had to, the second,
because they hated their apartment. Nowadays
we meet less often at their place. Several things
brought this about: G. left A.

(P.'s wife) and then M. (B.'s wife)
broke off with me, and the other M. (G.'s wife)
divorced G. and married me (while the B.s
also separated) and P. attempted suicide and
has been living more or less in a sanatorium ever since,
not to mention the changes in the world situation,
so anyway: there's nothing left to sit on.

(From the Hungarian)

GYULA ILLYÉS: TWO PROSE POEMS

I WORK

They stuck pigs in the throat. Might I not have done it my-self? They tossed chickens with their heads cut off out into the courtyard. With a child's thirst for knowledge, I watched their final spasms with a heart hardly touched. My first really shattering experience came when I watched the hooping of a cartwheel.

From the huge coal fire, with pincers at least a yard long, the apprentices grabbed the iron hoop, which by then was red hot up and down. They ran with it to the fresh-smelling oak wheel that had been fixed in place in the front of the blacksmith's shop. The flesh-colored wooden wheel was my grandfather's work; the iron hoop, which gave off a shower of sparks in its fiery agony, was my father's. One of the apprentices held the sledge hammer, the other the buckets. Places, everyone. As on shipboard. As at an execution. The hoop, which in its white-hot state had just ex-panded to the size of the wheel, was quickly placed on it; and they began to pry it out with their tongs. My father swung the hammer with lightning speed, giving orders all the while. The wood caught fire; they poured a bucket of water on it. The wheel sent up steam and smoke so thick you couldn't see it. But still the hammer pounded on, and still came the "Press hard!" uttered breathlessly from the corner of the mouth. The fire blazed up again. Water flung again as on a tortured man who has sunk into a coma. Then the last flourishing bush of steam evaporated while the apprentices poured a thin trickle from a can on the cooling iron which, in congealing, gripped lovingly its life-long companion to be. The men wiped the sweat from their brows, spat, shook their heads, satisfied. Nothing—not the slightest flicker of a movement— could have been executed differently.

(From the Hungarian)

II BRAZILIAN RAIN FOREST

In Old Buda, a street almost as wide as a square coming down from Újlaki Church. The one-story houses here are even lower than usual. The pavement once swelled to the level of the windows and remained there as in some frozen flood. From such a house, a tavern still privately owned, a tall slender young woman who is well-dressed comes out into the Friday twilight. Her eyes are glazed; she is dead drunk. She sways gracefully. The basalt cobblestones of the broad street mock her by pretending to be the stepping stones across a mountain stream, and that's why she may only step on every second one. Since the stones are wet, the scene is made all the more probable. It is raining, fully and evenly, as in the tropics, although it is November. The pouring rain is broken into threads by the light of the street lamps. The woman's disheveled hair drips also into so many threads. She is soaked to the skin.

She is soaked to the skin, but does not feel a thing. Otherwise she would not push away the threads of rain as if she were parting the reeds of a marsh or thrusting aside the bead curtain of some southern barber shop. But after this bead curtain comes another and then another, ten, twenty, a hundred, thousand upon wondrous thousand.

All this, of course, is illusion. The situation and reality: the woman walks amid the lianas, the hanging tendrils of a Brazilian rain forest, and above her are trees teeming with bright-colored parakeets, snarling monkeys, serpents, and other creatures that do not even exist in South America, but have come here only for this occasion. At such a time who would not think of coming to her aid? As Chateaubriand says, this is how the most exciting adventures with native women really begin. Yes, but there is something rarely taken into account—the distances in a rain forest! Between the two of us, my sailor's eye tells me, a thousand miles at least.

(From the Hungarian)

ANDREI VOZNESENSKY: FOUR POEMS

I SAGA

You will awaken me at dawn
And barefoot lead me to the door;
You'll not forget me when I'm gone,
You will not see me any more.

Lord, I think, in shielding you
From the cold wind of the open door:
I'll not forget you when I'm gone,
I shall not see you any more.

The Admiralty, the Stock Exchange
I'll not forget when I am gone.
I'll not see Leningrad again,
Its water shivering at dawn.

From withered cherries as they turn,
Brown in the wind, let cold tears pour:
It's bad luck always to return,
I shall not see you any more.

And if what Hafiz says is true
And we return to earth once more,
We'll miss each other if it's true;
I shall not see you any more.

Our quarrels then will fade away
To nothing when we both are gone,
And when one day our two lives clash
Against that void to which they're drawn.

Two silly phrases rise to sway
On heights of madness from earth's floor:
I'll not forget you when I'm gone,
I shall not see you any more.

(From the Russian)

II PROVINCIAL SCENE

While wind swept down the gorge as from the depot of the fates
I walked with my friend the quiet little streets
below a bakery sign in a sweet southern town.
Beside a blood bank a local vampire
leaned on the bumper of his car, awaiting clients.
My friend limped along, and bubbles from the earth
(or rather, bubbles rising between chinks
in the asphalt) came toward us like bums cadging drinks....

"You remember Annie, the little waitress, don't you?"

I did, of course. It was the astonished blue
of her eyes that distinguished her from her fellow hash-slingers.
She wore a braid, thought to be her own.
Had it not been for the gypsy violet of
her eyes, she might have modeled for Venetsianov.
She was always hurrying to her son with shopping bags of food.
Filled with such dark, golden strength
that any woman who saw her would grab her husband and
      disappear
as if someone had cried, "Look out, the tanks are here!"

Often when customers shouted, "Miss!"
her soul would freeze as if she mistook this
for some other signal, and then, waking up, would reply, "I'm
      coming, coming."

I remembered her clearly,
little Annie, the waitress—
she had slept with my friend, but not with me—
lived in a shack,
always hurrying to her son. Once the son
stood waiting, felt uneasy with us,
and clung to her like a pale vine; then he
kept watching us in the mirror
while pretending to study his Dante.

"You remember Annie, the little waitress? She's dead,
killed by her son for her money;
all that was left was her false braid."

So that is where you were hurrying, Annie.

"He beat her with a hammer while she slept,
the little clinging vine, the teen-age pimp."
My friend's teeth glittered in the wind.
"She was found by the sanitation crew
when her leg blocked their pump.
Her corpse was stuffed down the outhouse hole—
like in Shakespeare, bud, like a sinner in hell."

Over the night earth I saw her fly,
and "I've lost my boy!" I heard her cry
as she gazed in at the windows.
"He is not guilty!" I heard her scream.
"I hit myself with the hammer!
In the icebox there is sour cream.
Aren't you hungry, honey? I can't see my boy..."
and she tried to wipe away the excrement....

But the vile board surrounded her all the while
like the hatch of a conning tower or the nimbus of an icon:
In God's eyes nothing is vile.

"The whole town came to her funeral.
They guessed who'd done it. Suspecting him,
they said: 'Kiss your mother';
he refused.
And it was then that they found him out.
But he would not say who his accomplices had been."
"You were the killer!" I said to my friend.

Yes, Annie, you drowned in our minds
between news reports and dirty jokes...
heaven and hell do not exist—
you drift somewhere in between. Who are you now
in your new hierarchy?

A little scrap of nothing, are you? Stamen dusted with grief,
the rush of anxiety that comes before fog descends....
Where are you hurrying now, driven by what we do not know;
where in the world do you want us to go?

Sorry to disturb you for no reason.
Now in that ocean where one can't begin to count,
you have no doubt forgotten your thirty or forty years,
the fabric of provincial people, the initials in your ring.
But maybe you dimly remember their calls,
and for one second your soul may freeze,
catching a phrase that from a planet will descend.

"You remember Annie, the little waitress, don't you?"

The wind of judgment blows, the fateful wind.

(From the Russian)

III DO NOT FORGET

Somewhere a man puts on his shorts,
his blue-striped T-shirt,
his blue jeans;
a man puts on
his jacket on which there is a button
reading COUNTRY FIRST,
and over the jacket, his topcoat.

Over the topcoat,
after dusting it off, he puts on his automobile,
and over that he puts on his garage
(just big enough for his car),
over that his apartment courtyard,
and then he belts himself with the courtyard wall.

Then he puts on his wife
amd after her the next one
and then the next one;
and over that he puts on his subdivision
and over that his county
and like a knight he then buckles on
the borders of his country;
and with his head swaying,
puts on the whole globe.

Then he dons the black cosmos
and buttons himself up with the stars.
He slings the Milky Way over one shoulder,
and after that some secret beyond.

He looks around:
Suddenly
in the vicinity of the constellation Libra
he recalls that he has forgotten his watch.
Somewhere it must be ticking
(all by itself).
The man takes off the countries,
the sea,
the oceans,
the automobile, and the topcoat.
He is nothing without Time.

Naked he stands on his balcony
and shouts to the passers-by:
"For God's sake, do not forget your watch!"

(From the Russian)

IV   THE ETERNAL QUESTION

What more on this earth do you want from me?
Iron is the railing protecting your smile.
I am all discord, you are all harmony,
But the apple you offer's not from heaven but hell.

I have carried your name far across the sea,
And the purest of candles have lighted for you.
Your music brings joy, while mine brings decay:
What more on this earth do you want from me?

"You're pure?" you said, and, a serpent, I lied.
"Be brave, be a man!" So I slept with each whore.
"Be first!" you cried, and a genius I was:
What more on this earth do you want? What more?

I paid with my life till I couldn't pay more,
I died, and lay burning beneath your snowfall;
My words were of wonder, and you poisoned them all:
What more on this earth do you want? What more?

When they shoveled the last of the earth on my grave,
I still spoke no ill, and had only one claim:
That to freshen God's garden my bones might serve,
And if Error you are, then play your own game.

The mirrors behind you opened into a door,
And glittering, naked you stood before me.
"I love you," you said. "What more then of me—
What more on this earth do you want? What more?"

(From the Russian)

72

SÁNDOR WEÖRES: TWO POEMS

I VARIATIONS ON THE THEMES OF LITTLE BOYS

1

When I'm six I'll marry Ibby
And drive a big Mercedes—Ibby
Won't get in it—she can't come
'Cause she'll have to stay at home

2

CHARLIE IS A FOOL
JONIE IS A FOOL
    NOT ME—IM REEL COOL
    I got brains evry place—
LOOKIT— even up my ass

3

    Squads, right
    Squads, left
I lead the squad—Hup! Ha!
We're going to bury my Grandma!

4

Watch my Daddy build a house:
First the chimney puffing smoke
Next beneath it comes the roof
Then the windows front and back
Can't see through them they're so black
But you can see through the walls
Because they are not there at all
Now the walls are on their way
And one by one the rooms around
When the house gets to the ground
My Daddy cries, "Hip, Hip, Hooray!"

5

Tommy, running through the yard,
Catches Suzy, beats her hard—
Out of her beats the bejesus—
Then cuts her up in little pieces,
Strings her innards heart and liver
From one fence over to another.
Suzy's thinking: "This won't do
I will not let go of you.
Reassemble me, you fool,
Or you'll go to Reform School!"

6

On the house the sun shines bright
But in the sky there hangs night
And so Good Morning and Good Night

7

Peter and Pussy (begging your pardon)
Do nasty things in kindergarden;
Look at the pigs!
The other children stand and stare.
Teacher Abby says, "Look there—
Ugh, what pigs!"
Flashes her pointed pen,
Waves it in rage; Abby then
Writes: "Dear parents—dissipated lot—
Look what nasty kids you've got!
Can't you give us something better?"
Debauched parents then reply:
"Dear Abby: We sure try.
Now we marry, now divorce—
Makes all kinds of kids, of course."

(From the Hungarian)

II ELAN

Glides along midnight, holding up her lamp
in a light loose cloud, cut apart by light,
dances off on surf, russet-velvet clad,
veiled in purple air, seashore cutting in
below the mountain edge which the water bites,
runs off through the pines, to the clearing comes—
from where do you rise so the wind of the sea
never ripples your cloak, nor your shadow pass
on the ribs of the reef where the breakers break
nor your shadow touch the conical peaks
that align the shore nor the desert space
bear the print of your shape yet the clumsiest hut
is a place of love when you come there; where do
you go to, heavenly one? What do you intend?
What do you plan with our brushwood fire
whose flaming teeth never reach your steps
floating off above the wasps of fire, and the flaming
roses, leaving embers, cinders, cold, flying ash
only sorrow, desire, and black greed—O
naked reality of heaven, to what home do you call me?
passes to midnight, now into the clouds,
now beyond the clouds, topped with heaven's bowl,
now her space uncut, and herself not hid,
with no sleep her eyes and her heart no lid,
with her grace unwilled and her heat untold
with her words unsaid and her name unharmed
unblessed her desire to aid—not until
iron chains no more keep the bull's head down
and rats and snails guard the treasure trove
and children are fed on the blood of pigs
will the great goddess give up being cruel

(From the Hungarian)

LUKO PALJETAK:

BOX SHOWING WHAT THE WEATHER WILL BE LIKE

In a small pavilion lives a lovely lady;
a gentleman lives there in an adjoining room.
A model of propriety and comeliness,
gay she is in hat and trailing dress:
they walk together quietly each day,
the gentleman and the smiling lady.

He carries a black umbrella, always wears
a morning coat, cravat, thin trousers gray;
the lady smiles, a flower in her hair.
They leave the small pavilion where they live,
and take their uneventful walk each day,
the lady and the thin man with umbrella.

The gentleman goes out now only with the rain,
holding his umbrella, sedate and calm and slow,
the lady now emerges only with the sun,
lovely and smiling, a flushed and open flower;
but when a cloud appears she hides once more,
and the gentleman comes out as quietly as before.

And she goes out again when it is sunny,
brushing softly through the sweet young clover;
the gentleman remains at home, serene and lonely,
they emerge each day but never meet each other;
and when a cloud appears she hides once more,
and the gentleman comes out as quietly as before.

So slowly, in succession, the gentleman, the lady,
the gentleman, the lady, quietly they appear,
he with his black umbrella, she always alone;
the slow days pass, they cannot meet it's clear:
in the small pavilion where their lives are led,
invisibly bound as by the thinnest thread.

(From the Serbo-Croatian)

Part Two

OF ISLANDS

[1947]

THE PEACOCK OF JAVA

I thought of the mariners of Solomon,
Who, on one of their long voyages, came
    On that rare bird, the peacock
    Of Java, which brings, even
To the tree of heaven, heaven.

How struggling upward through the dark
    Lianas, they beheld the tree,
    And in the tree, the fan
That would become a king's embroidery.

How they turned and on the quiet
    Water then set sail
    For home, the peacock's tail
Committed to the legends of the sea.

3 FOR 25

Downing his drink to toasts of cut-rate jokes,
The sailor on the 10-day leave, the Machinist's Mate
2nd, squares his tousled halo for the folks,
And looks into the camera as at fate.
There where the painted palm tree's tonic sway
Recedes, authentic as a tourist folder,
Vast bridges spanning a blue bay,
As real as horseshoes float back from his shoulder.

10 days is not enough; but the Machinist's Mate
2nd leaves of his life this urgent pose,
These meerschaum fingers, eyes like dominoes:
And this one act, like all his holiday,
Is right only if he remains in black and white
When camera clicks with quick, conclusive fact.

THE MASSACRE OF THE INNOCENTS

Because I believe in the community of little children,
Because I have suffered such little children to be slain;
I have gazed upon the sunlight, dazed, bewildered,
As is a child by nothing more than rain.

Not until I can no longer climb,
Until my life becomes the tallest tree,
And every limb of it a limb of shame,
Shall I look out in time, in time to see

Again those who were so small they could but die,
Who had only their vast innocence to give,
That I may tell them, pointing down the sky,
How beautiful it might have been to live.

O LOVE, O LOVE, THESE OCEANS VAST

He who has felt on his dark bed
  The pressure of the tides
Finds sunlight ebbing round his head,
  Morning on all sides.

Like all heaven the hound will eat from his hand,
  And the wave like a new-born foal;
Manes engulfing a green island,
  Lions court his soul.

Lions that walk the yellow sand
  On the blood of morning fed;
And he who wakes finds light, his land;
  Darkness, fleeing, fled.

ON THE ISLANDS WHICH ARE SOLOMON'S

On the islands which are Solomon's I sometimes see
A swift, black bird which on wild pepper feeds;
And having reached a mild satiety,
Casts off its song like a merry widow's weeds.

Rich in wisdom from the shady bed of time
The islands rise, and to our world belong.
The hills are hot, the shores are cool with lime:
Hop to my hand, dark beauty, stripped of song.

THE DIVING BELL

Like one endangered in a diving bell
I move submerged, alone in the open sea.
Alive in love, I move in a lonely bell,
Driven alone into the open sea.

Immortal is the murderer who works my lines,
And all this air of heaven to no good;
Works me in loops, loops me in liquid vine
And takes me to his tangled water-wood.

Lost is the voice of the dark in dark dissolving,
Lost in the somnolent surf, the summer-swell.
I move in this world in such sonorous weather
On ocean bed I break from broken bell.

A NOTE ON THE VANITY DRESSER

The yes-man in the mirror now says no,
No longer will I answer you with lies.
The light descends like snow, so when the snow-
man melts, you will know him by his eyes.

The yes-man in the mirror now says no.
Says no. No double negative of pity
Will save you now from what I know you know:
These are your eyes, the cinders of your city.

THE BARBER

The barber who arrives to cut my hair
Looks at his implements, and then at me.
The world is a looking glass in which I see
A toadstool in the shape of a barber chair.

The years are asleep. A fly crawls on the edge
Of a broken cup, and a fan in the corner whines.
The barber's hands move over me like vines
In a dream as long as hair can ever grow.

CUPIDON

"To love is to give," said the crooked old man.
    "To love is to be poor."
And he led me up his accordion stair,
    And closed his iron door.

"To love is to give." His words like wire
    Dragged the ocean floor.
"Throw ten of your blankets on the fire,
    Then throw ten thousand more."

His room was the prayer on the head of a pin.
    As clean as a diamond cut
Was the iron door which opened in
    And would not open out.

"To love is to give, to give, to give.
    Give more and more and more."
And the wind crept up his accordion stair,
    And under his iron door.

OF ISLANDS

Of all the islands sailing down the west,
Of islands sailing north and south and east,
It is not islands you remember best —
Or better, have forgotten least.

It is not land, the quick, sure touch of trees,
Not all the lusty continent which sense reveals,
Which floats upon the mind immense with ease,
And steals away as quick as darkness steals.

It is not islands. It is less than islands,
Land still land until at once you see
You have come upon a calm, enclosed lagoon
And earth in its entirety:

And since it is an interim of sea and air,
Even as islands ultimately are,
And the waves are clouds which crawl back up the sky
To overtake a star:

Then even if the land is land no man can mend,
Which salt nor sand nor star can clean,
This is the island which our lives defend,
Where life must end, and death put forth its green.

THE CLOSING OF THE RODEO

The lariat snaps; the cowboy rolls
    His pack, and mounts and rides away.
Back to the land the cowboy goes.

Plumes of smoke from the factory sway
    In the setting sun. The curtain falls,
A train in the darkness pulls away.

Good-by, says the rain on the iron roofs.
    Good-by, say the barber poles.
Dark drum the vanishing horses' hooves.

CELEBRATION
AT DARK
[1950]

CHRYSANTHEMUMS

I had, here in the room before you came,
A dark delight announcing as with drums
Your coming, and the closing of the door,
Upon a table top, obese and tame,
These lion-headed flowers,
Four chrysanthemums.

A painter would have loved them, and been glad
To have them within reach: to see
Is mad, and madness teaches
Nothing if not love.
Great kings lay murdered in the flower beds:
I had, upon a table in this room,
Their four crowned heads.

In life we are often lonely, wanting death,
A kind of love not quite
Like this, a somnolence of light,
A glory which is native to the sun,
A poem in the landscape brooded on.

Dark springs, how dark;
And from the world's four corners, flowers
Like the heads of shaven Danes,
Huge and listless lions' manes,
Look down upon us where we lie
In darkness now, and overpowered die
Of love, of love.

THE GIRL IN GLASS

"You've stood there long enough," I said,
"Combing your hair. The pyramids
Are built; the traveler back
From ruined Thebes, Luxor, Karnak,
Has told the tale." You stopped.
And then, with fingers weaving,
Both white hands
Infiltrating copper strands
Of hair, began again.

Began, and then the delta sands
Ran out; you were a star-
Lit bloom, a water flower
Opening hour after hour
As I lay watching you in bed,
And the lamp burned low, and coral-red.

A mermaid in a fable wanted
To become a woman, and was nailed
With diamonds to my wall;
So Love, beside a waterfall,
Broke off a branch of berries from a tree,
And planted it at midnight
In the sea.

"You've stood there long enough."

PERSIAN MINIATURE

Ah, all the sands of the earth lead unto heaven.
I have seen them rise on the wind, a golden thread,
The sands of the earth which enter the eye of heaven,
Over the graves, the poor, white bones of the dead.
Over the buckling ice, the swollen rivers,
Over the ravened plains, and the dry creek beds,
The sands are moving. I have seen them move,
And where the pines are bent, the orient
Grain awaits the passage of the wind.
Higher still the laden camels thread
Their way beyond the mountains, and the clouds
Are whiter than the ivory they bear
For Death's black eunuchs. Gold, silk, furs
Cut the blood-red morning. All is vain.
I have watched the caravans through the needle's eye
As they turn, on the threshing floor, the bones of the dead,
And green as a grasshopper's leg is the evening sky.

MORNING AT ARNHEM

I

From the cassowary's beak come streaks of light,
Morning, and possibility.
In the countries of the north
Ice breaks, and breaking, blossoms forth
With possibility; and day abounds
In light and color, color, sounds.

II

In Holland there are tulips on the table,
A wind from the north on the gray stones
That breaks the heart, and sits upon the shoulder,
And turns the mill, the pine cones.

Waking below the level of the sea,
You wake in peace; the gardens look
Like roofs of palaces beneath the water,
And into the sea the land hooks.

In Holland there are tulips on the table,
A wind from the north on the gray stones
That breaks the heart, and turns, with the mill at cockcrow,
Over the quiet dead, the pine cones.

III

From the cassowary's beak come streaks of light;
A wrought-iron angel mounts a weathervane; you might
Be anywhere in Europe now that night
Is over, and you see that life begins like this
In tragedy: in light that is entangled in the leaves,
And morning shaken from an angel's sleeves;
And you can turn to face the mouth
Of the great black lion of heaven,
The terrible, beautiful south.

THE PARK IN MILAN

The animals we have seen, all marvelous creatures,
The lion king, the pygmy antelope,
The zebra like a convict cutting corners,
Birds in cages, orioles and doves,
The sacred ibis with a beak like a gravy dish,
Tropical fish weaving a Persian carpet
For the dancing feet of sunlight, marvelous creatures,
Theirs is the kingdom of love.

                Love we have brought them
On a summer day, weary from walking;
Like children who cool their faces on piano keys,
We turn to the quiet park, the good, green trees,
And a wealth of animal being runs in our minds like music.

Like music all the miracles of being,
The flash and fire of sunlight and of sound,
The elephant in cage of muted thunder,
Zebras on the shaken, shaded ground.

Turning from them now like children turning,
We watch the city open like a wound,
With gutted church and bombed and broken buildings,
Girders like black bones that lace the void,
All we build through love through hate destroyed,
The world an aged animal that heaves and cries
Under the trees, the gay, green trees of summer.

Music fades; the streets are black with flies.

NUKUHIVA

Nukuhiva, the scene of Melville's **Typee,** *is one of the Marquesas Islands.*
The islanders whom Melville describes are now almost extinct.

For Stephen Spender

I

It was in time of war, and yet no war,
No sound of war, and scarce the memory of one
So terrible that none forget, troubled
Our passage, the ship's dark keel breaking
The phosphorescent water, foam riding the halyards.
Far, far, far from home, the sailor busy with the day's routine,
We came one morning where the mountains rose
Upon a semicircular and emerald bay,
And a few birds circled like a flaw,
To the beautiful island of Nukuhiva.

Here Melville came, pursuing and pursued,
An angry spirit in a lasting rage,
Came tracked by time and all its skeletal
Transactions, the decay of empires, tracked
By life and death, and worlds of lies,
To Nukuhiva, and the whaleback bay,
An animal that listens with its eyes.

Seaweed trailed from scupper-hole, and folded sail,
The whaler rode the water, and the sailor's gaze
Went out to greet the islanders, the great
Canoes tilting with stalwart oarsmen, and the girls
As gold as morning diving from the surf,
The scent of oil and flowers.

II

                    The ship's boat swung
From the davits, then the wildcat purr of motors broke
The circling silence, and the jumbled rocks ashore
Came nearer, steady, up, the whip and lash of waves.

This was a place that memory corrupts,
A tumbling house half-seen through green and mottled
Foliage. The Frenchman talked of Paris and of youth,
Of Suez and Arabia and the East,
While the furious sunlight beat upon the rocks,
And words crept out like lizards on the leaves—
Bird-song, wind-song, sun.

The horses waited, cropping the dry brown grass
By the open gate, the crumbling wall; we swung
Into the saddle, sunlight flecking the hooves.

What was the island then? And who will say,
The wind, the sun, the moon? So much is buried there
In what was scarce a century ago
The center of a commerce and a colony,
Amalgam of Soho and a Yukon town,
Where drunken planter strode, and trader dipped,
And the bishop like a fat persimmon sat
Under the green palmetto in the afternoon.

III

Up, up, up, we rode through trees and tangled vines,
Struggling as one struggles in a dream
Across a moving mass of melting snow,
Words fail, the trail is lost among the trees.
Up the temple steps, the chipped, black stone
Breaking the clumsy branches, horses' froth
Smelling of papaya and mango.

Winding and unwinding like a leash,
We came to the burial platforms, the plateau,
And heard the water crashing through the vines,
And heard behind us, upward from the bay:
Revenez, revenez! On avait des copains!
Always in a language that was never mine.

Nukuhiva, Hivaoa, Raiatea,
The islands and the names are poetry,
And they are spoken by the voices of the drowning,
By the voices of the men who are remembered
By the cold, white, lonely presence of the sea.

IV

Whatever we had come for lay behind,
And what we sought lay still ahead.
As we approached the beach, the west was red;
The pompoms of the sailors danced upon the waves
Like poppies on the distant fields of Brittany
Across the semi-circular and horseshoe bay,
And all the wailing places of the dead.

GALILEO GALILEI

Comes to knock and knock again
At a small secluded doorway
In the ordinary brain.

Into light the world is turning,
And the clocks are set for six;
And the chimney pots are smoking,
And the golden candlesticks.

Apple trees are bent and breaking,
And the heat is not the sun's;
And the Minotaur is waking,
And the streets are cattle runs.

Galileo Galilei,
In a flowing, scarlet robe,
While the stars go down the river
With the turning, turning globe,

Kneels before a black Madonna
And the angels cluster round
With grave, uplifted faces
Which reflect the shaken ground

And the orchard which is burning,
And the hills which take the light;
And the candles which have melted
On the altars of the night.

Galileo Galilei
Comes to knock and knock again
At a small secluded doorway
In the ordinary brain.

MISERERE

The lights have gone out in the School for the Blind,
    And all the shades are drawn.
    Sisters of Mercy move over the lawn.

Sisters of Mercy move into the mind
    With steps that are swifter than any;
    Light on each pupil is perched like a penny.

The lights have gone out in the School for the Blind;
    The flare on the runway dies,
    And the murderer waits with dancing eyes.

The murderer waits in the quiet mind,
    While Night, a Negress nun,
    A Sister of Mercy, sweeps over the sun.

VINCENT VAN GOGH

Walking at night in a hat fitted with twelve candles,
The painter came to the edge of a field, and a barbed wire
Fence, and that was all.
The corn was ablaze, and the sky caught fire.

The stars were extinguished; the painter died,
Blood from his hand running into the flower beds.
Here is the cornfield, swirling ear, and all;
And in the foreground, nervously applied,
An intricate maze of thin-sown poppyheads.

ELEGY

For Bateman Edwards, d. 1 Sept. 1947

I stood between two mirrors when you died,
Two mirrors in a dimly lighted hall,
Identical in all respects.
Two mirrors face to face reflecting endlessly
Reflection's end.
The wind that had been blowing died away,
Or in the distance seemed about to die.
I stood between two mirrors in the hall.

Outside, the wheels had cut the gravel, and the sun-
Flower nodded to the sun; the air was still.
The deer that browsed upon a distant hillside
Lifted his antlers like a coral tree
Forgotten in midsummer undersea.
And from the delicate dark bridges which the spider
Spun from branch to branch,
In desolation hung
One leaf, announcing autumn to the world.

The world that evening was a world of mirrors
Where two great dragons from opposing caves,
Mirror their eyes and mirror all the scales
Of their long bodies and their giant tails,
Emerged. And all that had seemed human was confined
In terror in the limits of the mind,
And coiled, uncoiled within my memory.

In your sudden dying you became the night
Which I must add to darkness now
To make the morning bright,
To have day break, and daybreak
Melt the mirrors. But I know
You cannot hear me now although
I say, dear friend, good morning and good night.

EVENING AT GRANDPONT

Who under a stone bridge in the dark
Has seen? — We saw there, remember, wait,
The wind falls, wait, the street
Is empty now the leaves, the leaves
Are flocking to your feet —

Two swans, their floating, fluted necks
Down under feathers' whiteness,
Snow-plumed birds, awake? — No,
Not awake, two birds there deep
Down under thunder rocking,
Cradled, swans asleep.

Tell me, will you? — Well I know
How deep the swirling waters go
Beneath those two white throats,
The floor that whirls with dancer's step,
And death's dark notes,
Now tell me —

      Who
Under a stone bridge in the
Darkness? — Wait, the wind, the columned air,
The leaves are falling, and they gather there
Like China's universities before the gate.

MARTHA'S VINEYARD

The valleys of this earth patrol the sky;
Her mountains are the mountains on the moon.
Below us here the first white flowers die;
They all will soon.

Greater than life is love, and cannot end
Even in immortality; we take
Dimension from the force which made the moon,
The earth, quake.

Like roses we have seen in early morning
Sweeping a stone wall, spilling upon the ground,
Loves creates itself, or, dying small,
Accepts life's wound.

MARINE

A boat is cutting into the sea,
The children all cry, "Look!"
Earth and air are closing in
Like the pages of a book.

The day is brighter than hammered tin,
The breeze, a Mexican broom,
Dusts the air, the flying fin;
The gay umbrellas bloom.

Down comes the wave, up goes the gull,
Out goes the fisherman's hook;
Earth and air are closing in
Like the pages of a book.

White is the bone of the parrot fish,
And the jawbone of the whale;
Anemones in a cut-glass dish
Are not so deathly pale.

A hurricane lamp from far away
Burns in the little room;
And the shutters flap like hammered tin;
The distant breakers boom.

On the edge of the rock, the yellow sand,
In the shade of the leaning tower;
The children dream of the sea, the sea,
A blue cut-flower.

DREAM

One day in a dream as I lay at the edge of a cliff,
The black water rose, and the children bobbed in the street.
Death with her bonfires signaled the planes to land
Where glass-beaked birds had pecked at my bound feet.

The water's bare hands reached round the base of the cliff,
And my heart cried, "Hope!" and my brain, "There is nothing
     unknown."
I looked at my charts, and my kingdoms lay buried in sand,
My desiccate body picked clean as a bird's breastbone.

The ships for the west weighed anchor; I watched them depart.
And on what impossible port were their prows then set,
That they moved with a grace defying the mind and the heart,
With tackle of cloud, with decks encumbered and wet?

The air was like chalk; I was nothing. I thought I had
Reached the end of my dream; and I might have if
The waves had not risen and roared, the winds gone mad—
And when I awoke I lay at the edge of a cliff.

INDEPENDENCE DAY

Life is inadequate, but there are many real
    Things of beauty here: the flower peddler's cart
Adrift like an island in the city streets,
    The peddler's mare, lifting her mighty hoof
Aware of all that beauty. And the slate
    Where the schoolboy draws his forty-eight
States, ready to make room for the world.
    The sea's enormous wealth; societies
Commemorating blizzards in the North; the small
    White birds in the South where trees are tall
And the hoopsnake bounces downhill like a wagon wheel.

There are real things of beauty; all
    These things were yours. The shadowy
And fabulous quality of the imaginary
    Is presumed; we know it shall
One day take the world. Now the sea
    Has but poor mimic in the shell; a bell
Must free itself of sound, must break with freedom
    To be free. And so you broke, and so you waved
Farewell to us, and turned away
    To a mirror of completion and of certainty,
To clocks that tick, and have no time to tell.

Poems are praise, and poems cannot end.
    There is no answer for we do not ask.
Upon a cliff of sadness the trees bend
    Strangely toward the sea; the end
Is in oneself. O our unsuffering, suffering
    Sick friend, so life is adequate
And you are whole? There are real things of beauty
    Here, and sorrow is our praise. The day
Is bright, the cloud bank white with gulls.
    And while we lie, and watch the ocean roll,
The wind, an Indian paintbrush, sweeps the sky.

LACHRYMAE CHRISTI

Let the redbird come to feast.
The cherry-pickers long have ceased,
And I can see their ladders there
All aslant the summer air,
Heavy on the shining trees.
They bear away the jewel box
With steps like fingers winding clocks
That have not ticked for centuries.
Time is dead: there is no time.
No one now can ever climb
The ladder back to that black bough.
One man did, and he is dead;
And all the woods around are red,
And through the trees the redbirds fly,
While the rain falls from the cold sky.

THE WOOING LADY

Once upon the earth at the midnight hour,
When all the bells are ringing in the wood,
A lady lies alone in a palace tower,
And yet must woo, and yet must still be wooed.

She glides upon the stair, a bird on water,
In costly sable clad, in seven sins,
To lie beside her knight, a king's white daughter,
A scullery maid beneath the marten skins.

The stars are out, and all the torches lit.
Below the window is an orange tree,
Catching the light and then returning it,
A juggler in an antique tapestry.

Horses gallop away; the boughs are shaken
So gently it can hardly be believed.
And over all the world the birds awaken
As he awakens, beautifully deceived.

LONDON

Temptation, oh, temptation, sang the singers,
And the river passed them by like Banquo's ghost.
Deliver us from evil, and the river;
All are lost.

Salvation, oh, salvation, sang the singers,
And the ribs that rose and fell were barrel staves;
And I saw beyond the mist, the magic circle,
The hungry waves.

The river like a serpent moved among them,
And mingled, as it coiled upon each eye,
The faint, the dark, the scarcely flowing water,
And the quiet sky.

Death-in-Life is on us, cried the people.
Leaves from Birnam Wood are on the wind.
Holy, holy, holy, sang the singers,
All have sinned.

The stars have disappeared above the city
Like jewels from the crown of Banquo's ghost;
And London Bridge is falling, falling, falling,
Scaled, and crossed.

THE
DESCENT
OF
ORPHEUS
[1957]

LOVEBIRDS

Above finespun, unruffled sheets
Bright agitated parakeets
Do not well, encaged, endure
The changes in room temperature.

Heraldic in unstable air,
They seem inclined, impelled to share,
Through active beaks, frayed, busy wings,
Intense concealed imaginings.

They gaze beyond hot coiling pipes
And waving cloth of zebra stripes,
Past thicket-green, plum-colored walls,
Ape incantations, and bird calls,

To where abed, with swift intake
Of breath, the couchant lovers wake,
Muscles tensing, eyes agleam,
Within the alcove's rising steam.

Quadruped, engaged, complete,
The bodies there grotesquely meet
Until with dumb, direct transaction
They end in mutual satisfaction.

Above the tumbling, milk-white sheets
The red-green ruffled parakeets
Do not chatter, do not sing,
But perch, head beneath one wing,

Nor lift their eyes and gaze about
Upon the scene of such a rout;
How can rumpled feathers measure
Such accomplishment of pleasure?

While sated lovers lie apart,
Each sullen still-ballooning heart
Wanders high above their bed
To say requited love is dead.

Love, indeed, no longer here,
Mushrooms into the atmosphere
Until by some celestial curse
It breaks upon the universe.

It breaks—and planets on their round
Wheel unconcerned above the ground;
Winds attack hunched apple trees
And furrow snake-like, foaming seas.

The bed is made. The parakeets
Flash far away through tropic streets
In and out through black lianas,
Over broad sun-drenched savannahs,

Free and easy as the swing
And sweep of love's imagining
To where the temperature is even,
And the pure sunlight is all from heaven.

AMERICAN PRIMITIVE

Look at him there in his stovepipe hat,
His high-top shoes, and his handsome collar;
Only my Daddy could look like that,
And I love my Daddy like he loves his Dollar.

The screen door bangs, and it sounds so funny—
There he is in a shower of gold;
His pockets are stuffed with folding money,
His lips are blue, and his hands feel cold.

He hangs in the hall by his black cravat,
The ladies faint, and the children holler:
Only my Daddy could look like that,
And I love my Daddy like he loves his Dollar.

TULIP

A slender goblet wreathed in flame,
From Istanbul the flower came
And brought its beauty, and its name.

Now as I lift it up, that fire
Sweeps on from dome to golden spire
Until the East is all aflame:

By curving petals held entire
In cup of ceremonial fire,
Magnificence within a frame.

LETTER

Because a stamp will bear the damp
An envelope will bear a stamp.

Stamp and envelope unite
And fly together through the night

To reach the empty letterbox
A lean, uncertain hand unlocks.

Confronted with the cruel prose
Which stamp and envelope enclose,

Distraught, a young man bolts his door,
Paces up and down the floor

While metal rollers cross his brain
One hundred times, and then again,

Until as if congealed entire,
He kneels before a blazing fire

And sinks a knife into his heart.
Stamp and envelope depart:

Wet with tears, they rise in flame,
Leaving no address or name—

Only saffron ash that curls
Around dissolving blue ink-swirls,

Relinquishing to dark alone
Words written by the wind on stone.

REAR VISION

The cars in the mirror come swiftly forward,
While I, in thought, move slowly back;
Time past (reflected) seems to wind
Along the boundaries of mind,
A highway cold, distinct, and black.
Who knows to what the years have led,
And at which turning up ahead—
On the white-stitched road reflected back—
The furies gather in a pack,
While all the sky above burns black,
Unwinding still the darkening thread?

AT THE TOMBS OF THE HOUSE OF SAVOY

Turin beneath, on the green banks of the Po,
Lies ringed with bright sunlight, with peaks of snow,
While here in the dark this death's-head wears a crown.
The dead look up, and Death on them looks down,
And bares his teeth, his bone-white haddock eyes,
Which take the casual visitor by surprise
And follow him intently on his round
As fishbone-fine his steps through vaults resound.

THE DRESSMAKER'S WORKROOM

The dressmaker's dummy,
A mute flamingo,
Stands on one leg
For hours just so.

Around it in waves
Skirts billow and swish,
Thin squinting needles,
Slender white fish,

Dart in through shoals
Of blue-black moiré,
Crustacean scissors
Snip slowly away;

Stands while cock feathers
And marabou plumes
Beat the air brightly
Through darkening rooms,

Beads are set tinkling,
Lace makes the sound
Of a small wounded bird
Just grazing the ground,

Gold fringes quiver,
Button eyes stare,
Weird batlike swatches
Weave through the air;

The flamingo reposes,
The garment is sewn,
A shroud that encloses
Bird-feather, bone.

THE TEN

"... one of the best-dressed ten women."
—A newspaper reference to Mme. Henri Bonnet

Mme. Bonnet is one of the best-dressed ten;
But what of the slovenly six, the hungry five,
The solemn three who plague all men alive,
The twittering two who appear every now and again?

What of the sexual seven who want only to please,
Advancing in unison down the hospital hall,
Conversing obscenely, wearing no clothing at all,
While under your sterile sheet you flame and freeze?

What will you say of the weird, monotonous one
Who stands beside the table when you write,
Her long hair coiling in the angry light,
Her wild eyes dancing brighter than the sun?

What will you say of her who grasps your pen
And lets the ink run slowly down your page,
Throws back her head and laughs as from a cage:
"Mme. Bonnet is one, you say? ... And then?"

INTERIOR

He took the universe into his room
And shut the door;
Planets circled round his wall,
Stars along the floor
Rose and fell with the grave, slow-breathing dark;
Comets swam like the teeth of the swimming shark,
Beams of oak had monstrous ears,
And jackal's bark.

Sea birds came from distant
Islands; frigates, terns
Preened in the low revolving light
Their sea-bright feathers—wheeling,
Crying, darting down
Toward flickering shoals
Through the long night.

Past and future, two lean panthers
Black as coal,
Paced out the limits of his brain,
His life's veined ore;
And he could see
Gates opening before him quietly
Upon a rose-banked carriage waiting in the rain.

A PAVANE FOR THE NURSERY

Now touch the air softly,
Step gently. One, two...
I'll love you till roses
Are robin's-egg blue;
I'll love you till gravel
Is eaten for bread,
And lemons are orange,
And lavender's red.

Now touch the air softly,
Swing gently the broom.
I'll love you till windows
Are all of a room;
And the table is laid,
And the table is bare,
And the ceiling reposes
On bottomless air.

I'll love you till Heaven
Rips the stars from his coat,
And the Moon rows away in
A glass-bottomed boat;
And Orion steps down
Like a diver below,
And Earth is ablaze,
And Ocean aglow.

So touch the air softly,
And swing the broom high.
We will dust the gray mountains,
And sweep the blue sky;
And I'll love you as long
As the furrow the plow,
As However is Ever,
And Ever is Now.

A GREEN PLACE

I know a place all fennel-green and fine
Far from the white icecap, the glacial flaw,
Where shy mud hen and dainty porcupine
Dance in delight by a quivering pawpaw;

Dance by catalpa tree and flowering peach
With speckled guinea fowl and small raccoon,
While the heron, from his perforated beach,
Extends one bony leg beyond the moon.

I know a place so green and fennel-fine
Its boundary is air; and will you come?
A bellflower tinkles by a trumpet vine,
A shrouded cricket taps a midget drum.

There blue flies buzz among the wild sweet peas;
The water speaks: black insects pluck the stream.
May-apples cluster there by bearded trees,
Full-skirted dancers risen from a dream.

Birds call; twigs crackle; wild marsh grasses sway;
Will you come soon, before the cold winds blow
To swirl the dust and drive the leaves away,
And thin-ribbed earth pokes out against the snow?

ROBERT FROST: THE ROAD TAKEN

The poet stopped on the edge of night,
    And the road through dark wound on.
Black trees arose; the wind was still;
Blind skeletal walls inched over the hill
    In the mole-gray dawn.

He thought of the way by which he had come,
    Mastered through long years—
Tangles of form and substance, dense
Thickets past which with experience
    A writer steers.

He gazed beyond the familiar night
    On the reasons reason curbs—
Adjectives which say too little,
Adverbs that flare, or with dust settle
    On shining verbs.

A dim house ahead, a journey completed,
    Out of darkness, dawn.
The blind walls move: his words awaken
Here on the page; and the road taken
    Winds on.

IN MEMORIAM WALLACE STEVENS

One summer day a blackbird sang
Perched on the back of a great white whale;
Beautiful things by nature fail.

The whale submerged; a sudden gale
Swept the coast: the blackbird flew
Away with sunlight on his tail.

Montezuma, the blackbird sang,
Of lost Atlantis spoke the whale;
Only the cold wave sprang to view.

Against that wild and whirling blue,
A small blackbird, a great white whale,
A mariner shrouded in his sail

And all the blue thoughts that he sang
Are things which must by nature fail,
But, being beautiful, are true.

NIGHTWOOD

Seeking in squalor lean, elusive youth,
The pale quean haunts the bars, the murky streets,
Moving from love to love to love to love,
And loving but the self that Love defeats:

And loving but the robin and the wren
That hop from stone to stone on splintered legs,
And do not touch the hearts of buried men,
While clothed in soft, white light, the dark wolf digs.

A ROOM IN THE VILLA

What is the mirror saying with its O?
What secret does the still, untroubled surface lock?
What terror told by chair, by unmade bed and bedclothes?
    Now the clock is speaking; hear the clock.

Hear it tensely ask: Is someone coming?
Did someone just then step into the hall below?
Is someone there upon the stairway, whistling, humming?
    The solemn mirror's mottled, mocking O,

Like some black lake, absorbs all things in silence.
A tattered curtain flaps; the coals within the grate
Are kindled to a brief and unremarked refulgence
    While, patient in the eaves, the shadows wait.

DEATH OF A JAZZ MUSICIAN

I dreamed that when I died a jukebox played,
And in the metal slots bright coins were laid;
Coins on both my eyes lay cold and bright
As the boatman ferried my thin shade into the night.

I dreamed a jukebox played. I saw the flame
Leap from a whirling disk which bore my name,
Felt fire like music sweep the icy ground—
And forward still the boatman moved, and made no sound.

THE DESCENT OF ORPHEUS

Phi Beta Kappa Poem, Columbia, 1951

A cockatoo with nervous, quick cockade
Consumes the cones upon a tree of fire
Whose branches cast a giant, trembling shade
Upon the earth, and on the gilded lyre
Of Orpheus, who wanders underground,
And is consumed, and is consumed by fire.

Hear him, O wild singer, as he moves
Below the helmèd hills:
"We cannot live like this, we must empty
Ourselves of living: we must go down
Through Death's blue acres to the roots of things,
Life's darker surfaces, where huge hot springs
Break from stone.
                              We must seek Love
At the center of fire."
                              And through a tangled wood,
Past triple-branching flame, he goes.

Knowledge which is powerful will take
Man down those worn rock ways
Below the ground, into the dark god's
Kingdom, fire-dominion:
He must learn,
Like Orpheus, he cannot turn
But turning find
His sweet love vanished, and descend
Where days are nothing, and dreams end,
And broad and burning rivers flow;
And yet must turn,
And turning, ask,
"What shall I do without her?
                    Che farò?"

                    And wanders on
Beyond all light,
From total darkness into night,
Bearing his flaming shield, his lyre.

Here at the cave's gray mouth,
The grave's green edge,
We watch the cockatoo, and cry: Return,
Return to us among the living.
                    O so much
Is lost with every day: the black vanes
Turn in an angry wind, the roses burn
To ashes on a skeleton of wire;
Sun is mirror to the fire,
And earth, reflected, crumbles at our touch.

THE
TIN CAN
[1966]

MORELS

A wet gray day—rain falling slowly, mist over the
    valley, mountains dark circumflex smudges in the distance—

Apple blossoms just gone by, the branches feathery still
    as if fluttering with half-visible antennae—

A day in May like so many in these green mountains, and
    I went out just as I had last year

At the same time, and found them there under the big maples—
    by the bend in the road—right where they had stood

Last year and the year before that, risen from the dark duff
    of the woods, emerging at odd angles

From spores hidden by curled and matted leaves, a fringe of
    rain on the grass around them,

Beads of rain on the mounded leaves and mosses round them,

Not in a ring themselves but ringed by jack-in-the-pulpits
    with deep eggplant-colored stripes;

Not ringed but rare, not gilled but polyp-like, having
    sprung up overnight—

These mushrooms of the gods, resembling human organs
    uprooted, rooted only on the air,

Looking like lungs wrenched from the human body, lungs
    reversed, not breathing internally

But being the externalization of breath itself, these
    spicy, twisted cones,

These perforated brown-white asparagus tips—these morels,
    smelling of wet graham crackers mixed with maple leaves;

And, reaching down by the pale green fern shoots, I nipped
    their pulpy stems at the base

And dropped them into a paper bag—a damp brown bag (their
    color)—and carried

Them (weighing absolutely nothing) down the hill and into
    the house; you held them

Under cold bubbling water and sliced them with a surgeon's
  stroke clean through,

And sautéed them over a low flame, butter-brown; and we ate
  them then and there—

Tasting of the sweet damp woods and of the rain one inch
  above the meadow:

It was like feasting upon air.

SLAVE BRACELETS

I

You wore six bracelets—all of silver—and they moved on your
    wrist as you moved,

Catching the light, drawing it endlessly up and down in coils as
    you walked,

Bringing light in from the far corners of the room, bearing it
    in coils, cutting it in disks as you moved,

Peeling silver from mirrors, slicing the shadows; and when you
    held out your arm and drew it back,

The bracelets, tapping one upon the other, broke through the
    pebbled hours,

Slowly composing a pattern of continuing sound that I could follow
    clearly from room to room;

And the constant click of bracelets filled every crevice with silver.

II

A wash of silver! On that balcony overlooking the Caribbean I sat,
    and the water

Was a field of broken blue-green on which clouds massed and
    hovered in corners like paws,

And one triangular sail flitted and dipped, a checkered moth, over
    a crimson patch;

And the waves broke on a fringe of coral reef below, sweeping up
    over a circle of sand,

And the sound of breakers rose over my head, billowing out from
    the triangular tin roof protruding above the water,

Echoing dizzily through the green light; and below on the sand I
    followed the fine print of a crab darting in and out of his
    hole with every wave,

Tracing with each movement a slender radiating web, erased, then
    recomposed;

And again the combers climbed, and again your bracelets with
their tapping radiantly caught

In the tail of my eye; the sea became a battery of bangles, a
heap of polished abalone, uncoiling in profusion,

Splintering in silver at the day's dim edges, beached in delight
upon the afternoon

III

A fountain of energy had sprung up beneath my feet, and was
playing through my veins; the island

Moved with the sea breeze; abandoned windmills on the coral
hummocks turned in the imagination;

The ebony—that tree called "woman's tongue"—rattled its
dry pods;

The banana clattered its gaudy green leaves like so many machetes;
frangipani uplifted its clumps of coral branches;

Palm trees inclined; pawpaws trembled; wheelbarrows of fern,
guided by dark hands, came past

And the island was all in motion, but at rest; the sky, drifting off,
was caught at the edge of a cane field

By a grove of casuarinas, tall and feathery, planted in dark rows to
catch the rain,

Drawing water from the air to return it to the underlying levels
of the porous island,

Sweet water seeping down to rest, shimmering-clear, upon the
salt, filtering out through the cane, emerging in black pools
on the blond sand

So that all the island rested upon water—layer on layer—feeling
upon feeling—buoyant and balanced.

IV

With the continuous tapping of your bracelets, I began to compose
    a whole category of sinuous objects,

To detail an inventory of coiling images, of chains whose links
    rose slowly through consciousness,

Rivers meandering in mystical meadows, columns of smoke
    encircling unscaled mountains;

I followed with Australian tribes the parabola of the emu's egg
    across the sky—

Saw how, landing far off in a pile of kindling, it set fire to the
    sun;

I dug deep beside the legendary Papuan and uncovered with him
    the small bright object,

Which, slipping from our hands, climbed into the sky to become
    the moon.

I set out with Dionysus to visit the islands, and abducted with him
    by pirates, was tied with heavy cords

Only to see the knots loosen miraculously and fall to the deck;

Watched the face of the terrified pilot when he sensed that their
    captive was divine,

And the obdurate pirates still refused his release; saw the water
    darken about the ship,

Flowing freely into fragrant wine, while up from the deck, its
    branches enveloping the sail, a vine rose, looping its firm
    trunk around the mast,

And at my side, beneath great pendant clusters, under crisp,
    veined leaves

The god assumed his fearful aspect, and the sailors in horror leapt
    into the sea,

Where, as dolphins, they followed along in the somber water; and
    only the pilot survived.

V

Coils of sound uncoiling, loop on silver loop, circle of light on
    light—

Layer on layer! A crinkling serpent slithered through the shadows,
    nearer and nearer, always eluding me, twisting up through
    the mind's incalculable levels;

And I saw you then, a statuette poised against blue-green water,

A Cretan goddess, whose corsage exposed her small white breasts,
    her lapis lazuli, flounced blue skirts hooped over her waist,

Her arms extending rigidly down before her, serpents of gold and
    silver descending each arm into the resonant shadows,

Each neck held firmly between her fingers, the triangular heads
    thrust upward

—While the triangular tin roof behind you reflected the climbing
    breakers—

Each serpent clasped as if forever, its bright fangs reaching
    resolutely upward, uniting heaven and earth.

NORTHERN LIGHTS

I

I stepped out here on the mountainside, and saw the
  northern lights, cold-clear, clear-white, blue-green, long
  quivering gold knives of light shooting up, cutting the
  sky the horizon round.

Up from the valley mist rose in waves, shot up in steady puffs,
  clear-cold in the light,

And in places all the sky seemed made of moving skeins of white
  hair rising water-clear, stars tangled in the flowing strands.

The brook ran below (it was August, but cold); and I could hear
  its chill, pebbled water bubbling down, close in upon my ear.

Crickety night sounds: black trees came spangled forth, while
  behind a moving green gold turned them into shaggy hulks
  heaving in waves of light.

Trees stood, but moved, bearded and blowing, but no wind blew,
  and the dark itself moved, kept moving with light.

II

Mist, held deep in the valley in layers chalk-white, sheet-white,
  hung billowing between rock walls;

And still it rose, shade becoming light, light, shade, and as I
  stepped into the field, grass also moved, brightened by all
  these waves of hairy light.

The mountain pool caught, and tried to hold, patches of moving
  light, and the water, coming down from the mountain, rang,
  swinging clear

Over evergreens overgrown; ribbons of willow, beside or behind
  or above the pool, leaned, moved, kept clear-turning until
  the whole sky moved; and I stepped into an ever-deepening
  river of grass, green-moving and slow, glowworm-light
  expanding and wavering.

Thin blades of green cut through blue-green, or green upon white, white upon gray, green upon mist-yellow, green and prim-rose-yellow.

And primroses beside the rockpool, chill yellow in the moving mist; and light kept coming by while I moved with light moving, stood (leapt), reached (held) earth-air (whole-part), clear-cold and all-white.

III

I stepped forth, calm but much shaken: no night there ever had been so mist-torn, mountain-white.

The Milky Way had broken loose, and spun, a real web, round and round until the milk strands tore loose, and hung dangling above the valley.

A black dog lay by the road's edge, by a branch from a tree fallen, unmoving, shaggy with mist;

The dark barn jutted forth, its peak a prow, against the buffalo-humped mountains, and

In all innocence this night broke clear, sailing, sails trimmed and taut, no longer beclouded and cloud-tossed, but coming through, all clear.

IV

An August night: Jupiter off there in blowing, blissful mist-light.

It was cold; and sheer puffs, seemingly unpropelled, kept coming up and out until the whole sky was moving, nacreous and white—

All over mother-of-pearl, but pearl yet unformed, not white, but blue-rippling pearl-shell, caught up and streaming, moss-green, salmon-pink, and shaken.

Drunken, shivering, cold-quaking, I stood, moving skyward, still drinking deep draughts shimmering and milk-white.

146

V

The sky was a moving bowl, hairy and white, with the stars
chiselled and chipped, spinning in the whole sky.

And the sky was rinsed clear, while the brook rushed on below,
cleaving night sounds.

And the whole night moved, an upturned bowl, as if the soul itself
had been washed clear

Of all entanglements, and shone forth, fresh-clean, overturned
and opalescent.

It was as if the soul alone could speak, and having spoken, rippled,
rubbed, and crossed, had been drained of speech

And shone forth new-clean, clear-cold, and white, with nothing
now within to hold or hide ...

And I brushed the blowing skeins of light from my face, stepped
back and shut the door, and went inside.

AN OBSERVATION

For Marianne Moore on her seventy-seventh birthday

Now every day here at the height of summer
    from the edge of the apple tree bent by
    the weight of its fruit so that the whole thing

Is criss-crossed with strings of small green apples,
    looped every which way up and down and in and
    out—

Through the midday haze against the mountains swathed
    now in a gray-blue gauze of heat—

From the heart of the apple tree, its bark mottled and
    warped, its branches hooked and looking half-
    hollow—

From the hunched and dwarfed apple tree, and then from
    deep within the gray-green of the swamp willow—
    as if on a scale up and down its trailing
    branches—

Then high there on the bough of the fat bulging ash, its
    gold keys hanging dry and desperate like the fringe
    of old upholstery—

Now every day when all the other birds and even the
    insects have ceased I hear his chip-chip sweet-sweet
    chew-chew, followed by what sounds like a high *wit*—

Wit—which, as you know, somehow cuts through the heart
    of haze; and see him—a blue gem

Resting within the gray cushions of heat—his blue turning
    in the half-hooded light from indigo to ultramarine
    to azure,

Drawing into his faceted feathered body the gold and olive
    green of the mountains, absorbing as in watercolor all
    the lost color of the heavens

148

While below him dragonflies beside the elderberry bush dart
their wild blue brooches over the wet velvet surface of
the pond;

See him as you would see him, this New England visitor from
the coast of Cuba, this indigo bunting as more than a
mere jewel—

As a flame breathing at the core of consciousness, fed by
conscience, a poem poised against the shifting dull
gray seasons, asking, in its permanence and rare
felicity, "What are years?"

THE TEMPEST

Let England knowe our willingnesse, for that our worke is goode,
Wee hope to plant a Nation, where none before hath stood.
          —R. RICH in *Newes from Virginia*

Imagine that July morning: Cape Henry and Virginia
There but one week off; black winds having gathered
All the night before,
The gray clouds thickened, and the storm,
From out the wild Northeast, bore
Down upon them, beating light from heaven.
The cries of all on board were drowned in wind,
And wind in thunder drowned;
With useless sails upwound,
The Sea Adventure rode upon rivers of rain
To no known destination.
Bison-black, white-tongued, the waves
Swept round;
Green-meadow beautiful, the sea below swung up
To meet them, hollow filling hollow,
Till sound absorbed all sound;
Lashed about gnatlike in the dark,
The men with candle flame
Sought out the leaks along the hull.

While oakum spewed, one leak they found
Within the gunnery room, and this they stopped
With slabs of beef;
Their food they fed that leak, that wound,
But it continued still to bleed, and bled
Until its blood was everywhere,
And they could see their own blood
Rush to join it,
And the decks were wet and red;
And greater leaks sprang open in the hold.

Then, on the fourth day, having given up
All but themselves the ship contained—
Trunks, chests, food, firearms, beer and wine—

When they prepared to hack
The mainmast, to batten down all hatches
And commit the vessel to the sea,
They saw far off—sweet introduction of good hope—
A wavering light-green, brooding calm,
Trees moving with the waves—and it was land.

And so the ship rode on, rode out the gale,
And brought them, wrecked but living, to the island there,
Where safely, under more compliant skies,
They might chart out that voyage to a shore
On which the nation they had planted would in time arise.

THE LOVERS

Above, through lunar woods a goddess flees
Between the curving trunks of slender trees;
Bare Mazda bulbs outline the bone-white rooms

Where, on one elbow, rousing by degrees,
They stare, a sheet loose-folded round their knees,
Off into space, as from Etruscan tombs.

DACHSHUNDS

"The deer and the dachshund are one."
    WALLACE STEVENS, *"Loneliness in Jersey City"*

The Dachshund leads a quiet life
    Not far above the ground;
He takes an elongated wife,
    They travel all around.

They leave the lighted metropole;
    Nor turn to look behind
Upon the headlands of the soul,
    The tundras of the mind.

They climb together through the dusk
    To ask the Lost-and Found
For information on the stars
    Not far above the ground.

The Dachshunds seem to journey on:
    And following them, I
Take up my monocle, the Moon,
    And gaze into the sky.

Pursuing them with comic art
    Beyond a cosmic goal,
I see the whole within the part,
    The part within the whole;

See planets wheeling overhead,
    Mysterious and slow,
While Morning buckles on his red,
    And on the Dachshunds go.

PIDGIN PINCH

Joe, you Big Shot! You Big Man!
You Government Issue! You Marshall Plan!

Joe, you got plenty Spearmint Gum?
I change you Money, you gimme Some!

Joe, you want Shoe-Shine, Cheap Souvenir?
My Sister overhaul you Landing Gear?

Joe, you Queer Kid? Fix-you Me?
Dig-Dig? Buzz-Buzz? Reefer? Tea?

Joe, I find you Belly Dance,
Trip Around the World—Fifty Cents!

Joe, you got Cigarette? Joe, you got Match?
Joe, you got Candy? You Sum-Bitch,

You think I Crazy? I waste my Time?
I give you *Trouble?* Gimme a *Dime!*

QUAIL IN AUTUMN

Autumn has turned the dark trees toward the hill;
The wind has ceased; the air is white and chill.
Red leaves no longer dance against your foot,
The branch reverts to tree, the tree to root.

And now in this bare place your step will find
A twig that snaps flintlike against the mind;
Then thundering above your giddy head,
Small quail dart up, through shafting sunlight fled.

Like brightness buried by one's sullen mood
The quail rise startled from the threadbare wood;
A voice, a step, a swift sun-thrust of feather
And earth and air come properly together.

THE ANGRY MAN

El sueño de la razón produce monstruos.
—GOYA

I

Reason slumbers; and in the terrible isolation of my anger I observe a thousand monsters of the mind's making;

I wander on a moonscape exploring its tunnels, picking up bits and pieces of the past

To hurl at growling beasts that sulk away half-seen; I gaze from a steel cage out at a wall rimmed with dragons' teeth, observation towers and aprons of barbed wire

Lacing the horizon; eyes peer through the night as through the isinglass of old coal stoves;

I am a passenger on a ship in the shape of a carving block bearing a cargo of bones;

I know the language spoken by cats and dogs, all peripheral tongues; I invent new words, every syllable detailing disaster;

I am the King of Buttons, enriched by bottle-caps, profligate with paper;

My voice goes out like a funicular over an abyss, and my hands hang at my side, clenching the void;

My dreams are filled with bitter oranges and carrots, signifying calumny and sorrow;

And when I awake the windows are outlined in creosote; a network of pipes is thrown up around my room and water pours from a yellow geyser in the plaster.

II

Reason slumbers; and I go where the world takes me — back upon myself; and if I have slept, I awake, projected on a raft into a soft green landscape

Where blanched concrete highways keep circling the hillsides in
whalebone, drinking up the cars through the baleen formed
by spiny trees against the sunset—

And I am the passenger hurled from the passing car, the driver
swallowed by the black whale of the world;

And the journey ends where it began: the black whale's mouth
opens around me into a pleated camera in which my eye is the
lens—

And what I see is a world opening into other black mouths—
gullet to gullet—lens to lens—

And what is recording is recorded, what is seeing, seen; and
the giant shutter opens always on horror.

III

The monsters of the mind's making have begun their destruction
and will carry it through;

They keep attacking, throwing iron hoops that encircle my
ankles, thighs, chest

Until I am bound with iron rope and hung from a precipice; and
the cliff is no cliff but a ceiling from which hairy roots
dangle at my side—

Not roots but the branches of trees growing into the air by their
roots—

Around them dream flowers twisting out—black roses, blue sun-
flowers following a black sun—

Morning glories, dirt-colored blooms encircling mansarded
basements—

Skylights opening out like trapdoors into gray cloud caverns in
which birds dive downward like fish, and television aerials
float, the skeletons of dangling kites—

Rivers are nailed above me, their bird-fish flying, teeth dragging
    the marbled water, and their debris lining a painted dome of
    tin cans, bottles, rusted and twisting knives;

A bloated piano like a black armadillo bores its way over the
    edges into a cloud

And cemeteries drift overhead like upturned trays held by frozen
    waiters.

IV

The black iron hoops snap and uncoil, coiling me upward, upright,
    backward in time and space;

I am alone in a courtyard in the middle of a desert, holding in my
    hands the coils that have become a whip.

It is dusk, and the air is alive with soft flying creatures;
    I snap the whip at them, looping their bodies, bringing
    them down until the stones of the courtyard are red

And at last the air is quiet and no chirp or whimper is heard
    from any chink or crevice.

I climb the spiral stone steps to a room overlooking the desert;
    and I lie now on an iron cot watching the moon-white sand
    billow out in waves like the sea;

And the whip, having answered unreasoning reason, rests limp
    at my side—a tassel, a tail, a reed.

A PICTURE OF HER BONES

I saw her pelvic bones one April day
After her fall—
Without their leap, without their surge or sway—
I saw her pelvic bones in cold X ray
After her fall.
She lay in bed; the night before she'd lain
On a mat of leaves, black boulders shining
Between the trees, trees that in rain pitched every which way
Below the crumbling wall,
Making shadows where no shadows were,
Writing black on white, white on black,
As in X ray,
While rain came slowly down, and gray
Mist rolled up from the valley.
How still, how far away
That scene is now: the car door
Swinging open above her in the night,
A black tongue hanging over
That abyss, saying nothing into the night,
Saying only that white is black and black is white,
Saying only that there was nothing to say.
No blood, no sound,
No sign of hurt nor harm, nothing in disarray,
Slow rain like tears (the tears have dried away).
I held her bare bones in my hands
While swathed in hospital white she lay;
And hold them still, and still they move
As, tall and proud, she strides today,
The sweet grass brushing her thighs,
A whole wet orchard mirrored in her eyes;—
Or move against me here—
With all their lilt, their spring and surge and sway—
As once they did that other April day
Before her fall.

THE IDIOT BELOW THE EL

From summer's tree the leopard leaves are torn
Like faces from the windows of the train,
And at my foot a mad boy's tweed cap falls,
And no moth's born that can disturb his brain.

The traffic, with a sound of cap and bells,
Winds into his ear; his blunted eyes
Are button-hooks, his tight lips twisted shells,
His fingers, candy canes to snare the flies.

Below, the leaves lie still in wind and rain,
And overhead the rails run on and meet
Somewhere outside of time: the clamor dies;
An iron hoop goes clanking down the street.

FUNERAL

Now he is gone where worms can feed
Upon him, a discarded rind,
God's image, and a thinking reed,
    In blindness blind

As any taxidermist's owl.
He who was tall and fleet and fair
Is now no more; the winds howl,
    The stones stare.

Your double who went dressed in black
And beat the lions to their cage
Lies in blood; the whips crack,
    The beasts rage.

Don your somber herringbone
And clap your top hat to your head.
The carriage waits; the axles groan;
    While prayers are said,

Rest your hot forehead on the plush;
And hear, beyond the measured, sad
Funereal drums, above the hush,
    The lions pad

Intently through some sunless glade,
The body's blood-fed beasts in all
Their fury, while the lifted spade
    Lets earth fall.

THE TIN CAN

One very good thing I have learned from writer friends in Japan is that when you have a lot of work to do, especially writing, the best thing is to take yourself off and hide away. The Japanese have a word for this, the "kanzume," or the "tin can," which means about what we would mean by the "lock-up." When someone gets off by himself to concentrate, they say, "He has gone into the tin can."
— HERBERT PASSIN, "The Mountain Hermitage:
Pages from a Japanese Notebook,"
Encounter, August 1957.

I

I have gone into the tin can; not in late spring, fleeing a stewing, meat-and-fish smelling city of paper houses,

Not when wisteria hangs, a purple cloud, robbing the pines of their color, have I sought out the gray plain, the indeterminate outer edge of a determined world,

Not to an inn nestling astride a waterfall where two mountains meet and the misty indecisiveness of Japanese ink-drawn pines frames the afternoon, providing from a sheer bluff an adequate view of infinity,

But here to the tin can in midwinter: to a sagging New England farmhouse in the rock-rooted mountains, where wind rifles the cracks,

Here surrounded by crosshatched, tumbling stone walls, where the snow plow with its broad orange side-thrust has outlined a rutted road,

Where the dimly cracked gray bowl of the sky rests firmly on the valley and gum-thick clouds pour out at the edges,

Where in the hooded afternoon a pock-marked, porcupine-quilled landscape fills with snow-swirls, and the tin can settles in the snow.

I have gone into the tin can, head high, resolute, ready to confront the horrible, black underside of the world.

Snow-murmur! Wind-dip! Heart-rage! It is now my duty to record, to enumerate, to set down the sounds, smells, meanings of this place . . .

How begin? With the red eye of the chocolate-brown rhinoceros?
    With the triple-serrated teeth of the pencil-fed monster with
    bright fluted ears and whirling black tail? . . .

There is a skittering and scrambling in the can: a trickle of sand
    and sawdust from a sack, wet leaves blown back, cracks
    spreading along the wall.

There is the chitter and clatter of keys, a smudge of pencils, a
    smear of time . . .

Stippled heaven! Snow-ruffle! Garnet-groove! Black water
    winding through snow-wounds! Ripple-roost!

Will the wilds wake? Will the words work? Will the rattle and
    rustle subside? Will the words rise?

A bluejay flashes by a window, the stripes of his tail, chevrons
    torn from a noncom's sleeve; and in the afternoon the snow
    begins.

First: a hush—pit-stillness, black accent of hemlocks up and down
    the mountain, mist in the valley thickening and deepening
    until it breaks

And the snow already fallen swirls up to meet the snow
    descending—sky-darkening, still-deepening, sky-hooded
    and whirling, flakes flying,

Houses settling sidewise in the drifts—winds wedging, snow-
    choked road lost, still-winding, earth white-star-carpeted,
    still-wheeling;

And in the tin can the same still, paper-white, damp emptiness.

II

A door opens—is it a door?—and a woman walks by in the tin
    can watering tropical plants that jut from the wall or spring
    from the floor, their leaves great green famished mouths,—

163

Feeding the fish, distributing specks to the seahorses in their tank
and meat to the turtle on his wet pillow;

Cats curling about her legs, she pats the dogs and caresses the
heads of the children, and the children open their green
mouths and grow upward toward the sunlight like plants.

A door opens: a woman walks by, and through her bobbing,
mud-colored glass watches the movements of my pencil,

And a record turns, a black hemstitched whirlpool, and the
woman wheels off in a trance of drumbeats, screaming of
need and nothingness and money;

And money like wet leaves piles high around my ankles, and I am
sickened by its smell . . .

Snow-madness! Leaf-mania! Green parabolas! In the tin can
there is no morning of revelation, no afternoon of appraisal,
no evening of enchantment.

In the tin can a small boy in a nightmare kicks one leg from the
bed overturning a glowing iron stove, and in seconds fire
sweeps through a city of tin cans.

I wake thinking of the boy, and all about me are the smoking
ruins of cigarettes; and the ashes descend through the half-
extinguished afternoon with the smell of burning flesh . . .

A weasel waddles along in a kind of trotting walk; a mole inches
up through darkness, his blind trail, the workings of
consciousness.

In the tin can I hear a murmur of voices speaking of the life in
other tin cans, of death sifting through them.

A vision of bodies blasted on the black earth; and I think of those
photographs my father kept from the Nicaraguan
Insurrection, was it? — that we played with as children on a
sun-spotted floor—

Brown bodies spread out over the jungle floor, the figures beside
them wide-eyed and bewildered, toy soldiers in ridiculous
stances in a meaningless world;

I think of the photographs rubbed vinegar-brown in the sunlight; and of how we placed them around us, lined our toy fortress with them,

And talked to one another through tin-can telephones, while from out the photographs the jungle's green arm tapped our small brown shoulders.

III

The tin can is circling with beasts: dogs howl in the night, cats sidle through slats in the tin, wet field mice hanging from their mouths;

I step in the morning over the entrails of rodents lying like spun jewels on the carpet, offerings to the dark gods.

And the dogs rise from their corners, their dirt-crusted rag beds, smelling of snow, sniffing the roots, digging the floor, and begin again to circle the can...

Bright flashes of morning! Blue snow-peaks! Fog smoking the valleys! Angels lighting the rubble! Children skating on a blue pond! Deer stepping delicately down through the pines!...

And always the face, the woman's face, brooding over all, rising from the earth beside me, disembodied; always the woman clean and classic as sunlight, moving about the room, sifting the dirt, watering the shadowy flowers, polishing the spotted tin.

I hear her speak softly; and there she is again beside me; and again the face turns, a small bat-face and the lips draw back in a red wound and shriek; and the room is filled with a smell of mould and money...

The woman turns, the bat-face again a woman's face blue with shrieking, and the woman walks to the end of the corridor, climbs a broad white stairway...

Leaf-fringe! Sky-tingle! Cloud-clatter! Earth-blaze! All my underworld crumbles; and I am left with the one brooding face, no face; with bat-wings folding the black air into a shroud.

IV

When am I to emerge? Dirt falls; eyes blur; memory confounds;
   multiple voices move furred and batlike round my ears;
   and then no sound—

Only the grating of a pencil over a page—an army of ant words
   swarming up to consciousness.

When will they break through to a bright remembered world, up
   through the top of the tin?

Snow-swirl—hemlocks hunching toward the window—gray-
   black shadow cutting over black, fan shaken over fan...

From here the windows open their white mouths to swallow the
   wind-driven snow.

And I remember salmon sky, fine-boned sunsets sweeping the
   spiny mountains; and I have seen the snow

In banks driven back from the road, the black edges scraggly and
   bearded, the snowbanks under the birches like milk from
   buckets overturned and frozen...

Will the words rise? Will the poem radiate with morning? Here
   where I see nothing, I have seen the Cyclops-eye ballooning
   over a frozen world,

The wide fringe of eyelashes opening on all existence, the single
   glazed dazzle of the eye watching,

And I have lived with my eyes—watching the watching eye, the
   eyeball swivelling in nothingness, a huge black moon in egg-
   white immensity.

And I have seen the edges of the tin can fold in around it.

V

O bodies my body has known! Bodies my body has touched and
   remembered—in beds, in baths, in streams, on fields and
   streets—will you remember?

Sweet vision of flesh known and loved, lusted after, cherished, repulsed, forgotten and remembered, will you remember my body buried now and forgotten? ...

In childhood we played for hours in the sun on a dump near a cannery; and the long thin ribbons of tin rippled round us, and we ran by the railroad track and into the backyard behind the asparagus and through the feathers of green our bodies touched and the strips of tin radiated their rainbows of light—

And our bodies were spiralled with tin and wondrous with light—

Now out of darkness here from the tin can, through snow-swirl and wind-dazzle, let the tin ribbons ride again and range in new-found freedom;

Let the tin rip and rustle in the wind; let the green leaves rise and rift the wondrous windows, leaving behind the raging women, and the sickening mould of money, rust, and rubble ...

And the words clean-spun and spiralling orbit that swift-seeing, unseen immensity that will never be contained!

A deluxe volume of *The Traveler's Tree, New and Selected Poems* by William Jay Smith, accompanied by a portfolio of three original woodcuts by Jacques Hnizdovsky, has been printed in a limited edition of two hundred copies, numbered and signed by the author and the artist.